The Essentia

MINI

All Mini Saloons, Estates, Vans and Pick-ups: 1959-1999

Your marque expert:
Mark Paxton

VELOCE PUBLISHING
THE PUBLISHER OF FINE AUTOMOTIVE BOOKS

Other great books from Veloce –

Speedpro Series
4-cylinder Engine – How To Blueprint & Build A Short Block For High Performance (Hammill)
Alfa Romeo DOHC High-performance Manual (Kartalamakis)
Alfa Romeo V6 Engine High-performance Manual (Kartalamakis)
BMC 998cc A-series Engine – How To Power Tune (Hammill)
1275cc A-series High-performance Manual (Hammill)
Camshafts – How To Choose & Time Them For Maximum Power (Hammill)
Competition Car Datalogging Manual, The (Templeman)
Cylinder Heads – How To Build, Modify & Power Tune Updated & Revised Edition (Burgess & Gollan)
Distributor-type Ignition Systems – How To Build & Power Tune New 3rd Edition (Hammill)
Fast Road Car – How To Plan And Build Revised & Updated Colour New Edition (Stapleton)
Ford SOHC 'Pinto' & Sierra Cosworth DOHC Engines – How To Power Tune Updated & Enlarged Edition (Hammill)
Ford V8 – How To Power Tune Small Block Engines (Hammill)
Harley-Davidson Evolution Engines – How To Build & Power Tune (Hammill)
Holley Carburetors – How To Build & Power Tune Revised & Updated Edition (Hammill)
Jaguar XK Engines – How To Power Tune Revised & Updated Colour Edition (Hammill)
MG Midget & Austin-Healey Sprite – How To Power Tune New 3rd Edition (Stapleton)
MGB 4-cylinder Engine – How To Power Tune (Burgess)
MGB V8 Power – How To Give Your, Third Colour Edition (Williams)
MGB, MGC & MGB V8 – How To Improve New 2nd Edition (Williams)
Mini Engines – How To Power Tune On A Small Budget Colour Edition (Hammill)
Motorcycle-engined Racing Car – How To Build (Pashley)
Motorsport – Getting Started in (Collins)
Nitrous Oxide High-performance Manual, The (Langfield)
Rover V8 Engines – How To Power Tune (Hammill)
Sportscar & Kitcar Suspension & Brakes – How To Build & Modify Revised 3rd Edition (Hammill)
SU Carburettor High-performance Manual (Hammill)
Successful Low-Cost Rally Car, How to Build a (Young)
Suzuki 4x4 – How To Modify For Serious Off-road Action (Richardson)
Tiger Avon Sportscar – How To Build Your Own Updated & Revised 2nd Edition (Dudley)
TR2, 3 & TR4 – How To Improve (Williams)
TR5, 250 & TR6 – How To Improve (Williams)
TR7 & TR8 – How To Improve (Williams)
V8 Engine – How To Build A Short Block For High Performance (Hammill)
Volkswagen Beetle Suspension, Brakes & Chassis – How To Modify For High Performance (Hale)
Volkswagen Bus Suspension, Brakes & Chassis – How To Modify For High Performance (Hale)
Weber DCOE, & Dellorto DHLA Carburetors – How To Build & Power Tune 3rd Edition (Hammill)

Those Were The Days ... Series
Alpine Trials & Rallies 1910-1973 (Pfundner)
Austerity Motoring (Bobbitt)
Brighton National Speed Trials (Gardiner)
British Lorries Of The 1950s (Bobbitt)
British Touring Car Championship, The (Collins)
British Police Cars (Walker)
British Woodies (Peck)
Dune Buggy Phenomenon (Hale)
Dune Buggy Phenomenon Volume 2 (Hale)
Hot Rod & Stock Car Racing in Britain In The 1980s (Neil)
Last Real Austins, The, 1946-1959 (Peck)
MG's Abingdon Factory (Moylan)
Motor Racing At Brands Hatch In The Seventies (Parker)
Motor Racing At Brands Hatch In The Eighties (Parker)
Motor Racing At Crystal Palace (Collins)
Motor Racing At Goodwood In The Sixties (Gardiner)
Motor Racing At Nassau In The 1950s & 1960s (O'Neil)
Motor Racing At Oulton Park In The 1960s (McFadyen)
Motor Racing At Oulton Park In The 1970s (McFadyen)
Three Wheelers (Bobbitt)

Enthusiast's Restoration Manual Series
Citroën 2CV, How To Restore (Porter)
Classic Car Bodywork, How To Restore (Thaddeus)
Classic Car Electrics (Thaddeus)
Classic Cars, How To Paint (Thaddeus)
Reliant Regal, How To Restore (Payne)
Triumph TR2, 3, 3A, 4 & 4A, How To Restore (Williams)
Triumph TR5/250 & 6, How To Restore (Williams)
Triumph TR7/8, How To Restore (Williams)
Volkswagen Beetle, How To Restore (Tyler)
VW Bay Window Bus (Paxton)
Yamaha FS1-E, How To Restore (Watts)

Essential Buyer's Guide Series
Alfa GT (Booker)
Alfa Romeo Spider Giulia (Booker & Talbott)
BMW GS (Henshaw)
BSA Bantam (Henshaw)
BSA Twins (Henshaw)
Citroën 2CV (Paxton)
Citroën ID & DS (Heilig)
Fiat 500 & 600 (Bobbitt)
Jaguar E-type 3.8 & 4.2-litre (Crespin)
Jaguar E-type V12 5.3-litre (Crespin)
Jaguar XJ 1995-2003 (Crespin)
Jaguar/Daimler XJ6, XJ12 & Sovereign (Crespin)
Jaguar/Daimler XJ40 (Crespin)
Jaguar XJ-S (Crespin)
MGB & MGB GT (Williams)
Mercedes-Benz 280SL-560DSL Roadsters (Bass)
Mercedes-Benz 'Pagoda' 230SL, 250SL & 280SL Roadsters & Coupés (Bass)
Mini (Paxton)
Morris Minor & 1000 (Newell)
Porsche 928 (Hemmings)
Rolls-Royce Silver Shadow & Bentley T-Series (Bobbitt)
Subaru Impreza (Hobbs)
Triumph Bonneville (Henshaw)
Triumph TR6 (Williams)
VW Beetle (Cservenka & Copping)
VW Bus (Cservenka & Copping)
VW Golf GTI (Cservenka & Copping)

Auto-Graphics Series
Fiat-based Abarths (Sparrow)
Jaguar MKI & II Saloons (Sparrow)
Lambretta Li Series Scooters (Sparrow)

Rally Giants Series
Audi Quattro (Robson)
Austin Healey 100-6 & 3000 (Robson)
Fiat 131 Abarth (Robson)
Ford Escort MkI (Robson)
Ford Escort RS Cosworth & World Rally Car (Robson)
Ford Escort RS1800 (Robson)
Lancia Stratos (Robson)
Mini Cooper/Mini Cooper S (Robson)
Peugeot 205 T16 (Robson)
Subaru Impreza (Robson)

General
1½-litre GP Racing 1961-1965 (Whitelock)
AC Two-litre Saloons & Buckland Sportscars (Archibald)
Alfa Romeo Giulia Coupé GT & GTA (Tipler)
Alfa Romeo Montreal – The Essential Companion (Taylor)
Alfa Tipo 33 (McDonough & Collins)
Alpine & Renault – The Development Of The Revolutionary Turbo F1 Car 1968 to 1979 (Smith)
Anatomy Of The Works Minis (Moylan)
Armstrong-Siddeley (Smith)
Autodrome (Collins & Ireland)
Automotive A-Z, Lane's Dictionary Of Automotive Terms (Lane)
Automotive Mascots (Kay & Springate)
Bahamas Speed Weeks, The (O'Neil)
Bentley Continental, Corniche And Azure (Bennett)
Bentley MkVI, Rolls-Royce Silver Wraith, Dawn & Cloud/Bentley R & S-Series (Nutland)
BMC Competitions Department Secrets (Turner, Chambers Browning)
BMW 5-Series (Cranswick)
BMW Z-Cars (Taylor)
BMW Boxer Twins 1970-1995 Bible, The (Falloon)
Britains Farm Model Balers & Combines 1967 to 2007 (Pullen)
British 250cc Racing Motorcycles (Pereira)
British Cars, The Complete Catalogue Of, 1895-1975 (Culshaw & Horrobin)
BRM – A Mechanic's Tale (Salmon)
BRM V16 (Ludvigsen)
BSA Bantam Bible, The (Henshaw)
Bugatti Type 40 (Price)
Bugatti 46/50 Updated Edition (Price & Arbey)
Bugatti T44 & T49 (Price & Arbey)
Bugatti 57 2nd Edition (Price)
Caravans, The Illustrated History 1919-1959 (Jenkinson)
Caravans, The Illustrated History From 1960 (Jenkinson)
Carrera Panamericana, La (Tipler)
Chrysler 300 – America's Most Powerful Car 2nd Edition (Ackerson)
Chrysler PT Cruiser (Ackerson)
Citroën DS (Bobbitt)
Classic British Car Electrical Systems (Astley)
Cliff Allison – From The Fells To Ferrari (Gauld)
Cobra – The Real Thing! (Legate)
Cortina – Ford's Bestseller (Robson)
Coventry Climax Racing Engines (Hammill)
Daimler SP250 New Edition (Long)
Datsun Fairlady Roadster To 280ZX – The Z-Car Story (Long)
Diecast Toy Cars of the 1950s & 1960s (Ralston)
Dino – The V6 Ferrari (Long)
Dodge Challenger & Plymouth Barracuda (Grist)
Dodge Charger – Enduring Thunder (Ackerson)
Dodge Dynamite! (Grist)
Donington (Boddy)
Draw & Paint Cars – How To (Gardiner)
Drive On The Wild Side, A – 20 Extreme Driving Adventures From Around The World (Weaver)
Ducati 750 Bible, The (Falloon)
Ducati 860, 900 And Mille Bible, The (Falloon)
Dune Buggy, Building A – The Essential Manual (Shakespeare)
Dune Buggy Files (Hale)
Dune Buggy Handbook (Hale)
Edward Turner: The Man Behind The Motorcycles (Clew)
Fast Ladies – Female Racing Drivers 1888 to 1970 (Bouzanquet)
Fiat & Abarth 124 Spider & Coupé (Tipler)
Fiat & Abarth 500 & 600 2nd Edition (Bobbitt)
Fiats, Great Small (Ward)
Fine Art Of The Motorcycle Engine, The (Peirce)
Ford F100/F150 Pick-up 1948-1996 (Ackerson)
Ford F150 Pick-up 1997-2005 (Ackerson)
Ford GT – Then, And Now (Streather)
Ford GT40 (Legate)
Ford In Miniature (Olson)
Ford Model Y (Roberts)
Ford Thunderbird From 1954, The Book Of The (Long)
Forza Minardi! (Vigar)
Funky Mopeds (Skelton)
Gentleman Jack (Gauld)
GM In Miniature (Olson)
GT – The World's Best GT Cars 1953-73 (Dawson)
Hillclimbing & Sprinting – The Essential Manual (Short & Wilkinson)
Honda NSX (Long)
Jaguar, The Rise Of (Price)
Jaguar XJ-S (Long)
Jeep CJ (Ackerson)
Jeep Wrangler (Ackerson)
Karmann-Ghia Coupé & Convertible (Bobbitt)
Lamborghini Miura Bible, The (Sackey)
Lambretta Bible, The (Davies)
Lancia 037 (Collins)
Lancia Delta HF Integrale (Blaettel & Wagner)
Land Rover, The Half-ton Military (Cook)
Laverda Twins & Triples Bible 1968-1986 (Falloon)
Lea-Francis Story, The (Price)
Lexus Story, The (Long)
little book of smart, the (Jackson)
Lola – The Illustrated History (1957-1977) (Starkey)
Lola – All The Sports Racing & Single-seater Racing Cars 1978-1997 (Starkey)
Lola T70 – The Racing History & Individual Chassis Record 4th Edition (Starkey)
Lotus 49 (Oliver)
Marketingmobiles, The Wonderful Wacky World Of (Hale)
Mazda MX-5/Miata 1.6 Enthusiast's Workshop Manual (Grainger & Shoemark)
Mazda MX-5/Miata 1.8 Enthusiast's Workshop Manual (Grainger & Shoemark)
Mazda MX-5 Miata: The Book Of The World's Favourite Sportscar (Long)
Mazda MX-5 Miata Roadster (Long)
Maximum Mini (Booij)
MGA (Price Williams)
MGB & MGB GT– Expert Guide (Auto-doc Series) (Williams)
MGB Electrical Systems Updated & Revised Edition (Astley)
Micro Caravans (Jenkinson)
Micro Trucks (Mort)
Microcars At Large! (Quellin)
Mini Cooper – The Real Thing! (Tipler)
Mitsubishi Lancer Evo, The Road Car & WRC Story (Long)
Montlhéry, The Story Of The Paris Autodrome (Boddy)
Morgan Maverick (Lawrence)
Morris Minor, 60 Years On The Road (Newell)
Moto Guzzi Sport & Le Mans Bible, The (Falloon)
Motor Movies – The Posters! (Veysey)
Motor Racing – Reflections Of A Lost Era (Carter)
Motorcycle Apprentice (Cakebread)
Motorcycle Road & Racing Chassis Designs (Noakes)
Motorhomes, The Illustrated History (Jenkinson)
Motorsport In colour, 1950s (Wainwright)
Nissan 300ZX & 350Z – The Z-Car Story (Long)
Off-Road Giants! – Heroes of 1960s Motorcycle Sport (Westlake)
Pass The Theory And Practical Driving Tests (Gibson & Hoole)
Peking To Paris 2007 (Young)
Plastic Toy Cars Of The 1950s & 1960s (Ralston)
Pontiac Firebird (Cranswick)
Porsche Boxster (Long)
Porsche 356 (2nd Edition) (Long)
Porsche 908 (Födisch, Neßhöver, Roßbach, Schwarz & Roßbach)
Porsche 911 Carrera – The Last Of The Evolution (Corlett)
Porsche 911R, RS & RSR, 4th Edition (Starkey)
Porsche 911 – The Definitive History 1963-1971 (Long)
Porsche 911 – The Definitive History 1971-1977 (Long)
Porsche 911 – The Definitive History 1977-1987 (Long)
Porsche 911 – The Definitive History 1987-1997 (Long)
Porsche 911 – The Definitive History 1997-2004 (Long)
Porsche 911SC 'Super Carrera' – The Essential Companion (Streather)
Porsche 914 & 914-6: The Definitive History Of The Road & Competition Cars (Long)
Porsche 924 (Long)
Porsche 928 (Long)
Porsche 944 (Long)
Porsche 964, 993 & 996 Data Plate Code Breaker (Streather)
Porsche 993 'King Of Porsche' – The Essential Companion (Streather)
Porsche 996 'Supreme Porsche' – The Essential Companion (Streather)
Porsche Racing Cars – 1953 To 1975 (Long)
Porsche Racing Cars – 1976 To 2005 (Long)
Porsche – The Rally Story (Meredith)
Porsche: Three Generations Of Genius (Meredith)
RAC Rally Action! (Gardiner)
Rallye Sport Fords: The Inside Story (Moreton)
Redman, Jim – 6 Times World Motorcycle Champion: The Autobiography (Redman)
Rolls-Royce Silver Shadow/Bentley T Series Corniche & Camargue Revised & Enlarged Edition (Bobbitt)
Rolls-Royce Silver Spirit, Silver Spur & Bentley Mulsanne 2nd Edition (Bobbitt)
Russian Motor Vehicles (Kelly)
RX-7 – Mazda's Rotary Engine Sportscar (Updated & Revised New Edition) (Long)
Scooters & Microcars, The A-Z Of Popular (Dan)
Scooter Lifestyle (Grainger)
Singer Story: Cars, Commercial Vehicles, Bicycles & Motorcycle (Atkinson)
SM – Citroën's Maserati-engined Supercar (Long & Claverol)
Subaru Impreza: The Road Car And WRC Story (Long)
Supercar, How To Build your own (Thompson)
Taxi! The Story Of The 'London' Taxicab (Bobbitt)
Tinplate Toy Cars Of The 1950s & 1960s (Ralston)
Toyota Celica & Supra, The Book Of Toyota's Sports Coupés (Long)
Toyota MR2 Coupés & Spyders (Long)
Triumph Motorcycles & The Meriden Factory (Hancox)
Triumph Speed Twin & Thunderbird Bible (Woolridge)
Triumph Tiger Cub Bible (Estall)
Triumph Trophy Bible (Woolridge)
Triumph TR6 (Kimberley)
Unraced (Collins)
Velocette Motorcycles – MSS To Thruxton Updated & Revised (Burris)
Virgil Exner – Visioneer: The Official Biography Of Virgil M Exner Designer Extraordinaire (Grist)
Volkswagen Bus Book, The (Bobbitt)
Volkswagen Bus Or Van To Camper, How To Convert (Porter)
Volkswagens Of The World (Glen)
VW Beetle Cabriolet (Bobbitt)
VW Beetle – The Car Of The 20th Century (Copping)
VW Bus – 40 Years Of Splitties, Bays & Wedges (Copping)
VW Bus Book, The (Bobbitt)
VW Golf: Five Generations Of Fun (Copping & Cservenka)
VW – The Air-cooled Era (Copping)
VW T5 Camper Conversion Manual (Porter)
VW Campers (Copping)
Works Minis, The Last (Purves & Brenchley)
Works Rally Mechanic (Moylan)

www.veloce.co.uk

First published in March 2009 by Veloce Publishing Limited, 33 Trinity Street, Dorchester DT1 1TT, England. Fax 01305 268864/e-mail info@veloce.co.uk/web www.veloce.co.uk or www.velocebooks.com.
ISBN: 978-1-84584-204-8/UPC: 636847042042

Readers with ideas for automotive books, or books on other transport or related hobby subjects, are invited to write to the editorial director of Veloce Publishing at the above address.
British Library Cataloguing in Publication Data – A catalogue record for this book is available from the British Library. Typesetting, design and page make-up all by Veloce Publishing Ltd on Apple Mac. Printed in India by Replika Press.

Introduction & thanks
– the purpose of this book

The world of classic cars is awash with overused superlatives – often applied to vehicles which were mind-numbingly mediocre when new, and only worthy of note today because their numbers have dwindled sufficiently to transform them into nostalgic oddities. The Mini, though, deserves every ounce of praise that it attracts because it was an inspired design, whose attributes are as relevant now as they were on the day it was launched. Never before had such an externally tiny package managed to provide so spacious a passenger cabin, and, for the technically-minded, it provided elegant and innovative solutions to problems that other manufacturers hadn't even started to address in 1959, and undoubtedly set a new standard for engineering excellence in small cars. Safe and predictable handling was designed in, and coupled to pin sharp steering which meant that the Mini could happily combine the roles of economic family runabout during the week and compact sporting saloon at the weekend. The icing on the cake was a timeless and ultimately classless styling which, although not exactly beautiful, was certainly cute and distinctive. The Mini was unique, and one of only a handful of cars to have been recognised as a 20th century motoring icon.

Nothing is perfect, though, and the otherwise excellent design unfortunately contained dozens of rust traps, and quality control during production could be patchy at best, but these failings were never going to be enough to turn the buying public away from the car.

If having a Mini grace your driveway is a dream that you would like to turn into reality then this volume will take you through a buying process that will weed out the obviously unsuitable, then move on to a step-by-step look at the more promising cars. Concentrating mainly on saloons made from the late sixties on – by far the most common on the secondhand market these days, though most of the information happily applies to all models and years – it will examine the most common frailties; both body and mechanical. The unique points system included

in the *Essential Buyers Guides* will help to ensure that you end up with the best example you can get for your hard-earned cash, and your very own Mini icon to cherish for years to come.

Mark Paxton
Warrington
England

'Mini'malist pretty much sums it up.

Contents

www.velocebooks.com/www.veloce.co.uk
All current books • New book news • Special offers • Gift vouchers • Forum

1 Is it the right car for you?
– marriage guidance!

Tall and short drivers
The Mini is renowned for its space-saving design which allows even the tallest of drivers to be accommodated, although those long in the leg may find that their knees have to be wrapped around the steering wheel, which can be uncomfortable over longer distances.

Weight of controls
The steering is light and positive, only tightening up slightly during low speed manoeuvres. Drum-braked cars need a firm foot on the pedal to extract maximum retardation; disc-equipped models, especially when aided by a servo, are fine. The clutch may feel heavy compared to more modern cars.

Will it fit in the garage?
If a Mini won't then nothing will! The Saloon is 3.05 metres long, 1.41 metres wide, and 1.33 metres high. The Estate, Van and Pick-up are all approximately 25cm longer.

Interior space
For a car with such tiny external dimensions the interior is remarkably roomy, although larger adults will find the rear legroom a bit tight. Headroom is fine, too, although it can feel claustrophobic in the back of cars with fixed rear windows.

Luggage capacity
The early cars are the best in this respect as they have large door pockets, courtesy of the sliding windows fitted, plus a boot lid which could be left open to extend the load area, thanks to a top-hinged number plate that pivoted down so it remained visible. All models have good dash space plus a couple of metal storage bins either side of the rear seat. The boot is not bad for the size of the car but would struggle on an extended touring holiday, so it's unsurprising that boot and roof racks were a common addition in the '60s and '70s when Minis were often used as the main family car.

Running costs
Certainly one of the cheapest cars to keep on the road, a Mini is thrifty on fuel, light on tyres, and very cheap to repair and maintain. Approximate fuel consumption:

1970s	850cc	48mpg
1980s	1000cc	45mpg
1990s	1300cc Injection	42mpg

Usability
Still an eminently practical car today. 850s are probably at their best in town and on quieter roads, but any of the bigger-engined Minis can still cut the mustard in faster traffic, although long motorway trips can be noisy in a 1000cc held at the legal limit. Soundproofing improved in the nineties, so later cars are much better.

Parts availability
Superb – it's possible to virtually create a completely new car from a mix of reproduction, replacement and old stock bits. Some items for the very early cars may need a bit more hunting down, particularly trim pieces, but it's still a much rosier picture than for most cars of the period.

Parts cost
Very reasonable – a vibrant market helps to keep things competitive. Occasionally, some early bits will command a premium, but there are reproduction parts coming along on a regular basis to fill any gaps.

Insurance group
It simply doesn't come any cheaper. Classic policies are the order of the day for most people now, as values have risen, although you may have to endure an annual mileage restriction.

Investment potential
Rarer versions, like early Coopers, command serious money, and will continue to appreciate in the long term. Standard Saloons from the '70s and '80s remain at the bottom of the pile but are unlikely to drop in value as long as their condition is maintained.

Foibles
Very few, as the Mini was a well-designed car from the outset. Wet weather can be trying as it can cause misfiring, leaks into the interior, and problems with misting up, but all of these can be successfully addressed with a little attention to detail.

Minus points
Can be leaky, as we've said, and not always the warmest thanks as much to a basic distribution system as any real weakness in the heater. There's no point in investing in a stereo on earlier cars unless it is loud.

Alternatives
There really isn't anything quite like a Mini. There are other classic city cars but nothing else with the unbeatable combination of everyday utility with rally level handling, timeless looks, and an appeal that transcends money and class.

2 Cost considerations
– affordable, or a money pit?

Small service ●x50
Large service ●x120
Reconditioned engine and 'box ●x1400
Reconditioned cylinder head (unleaded)
    ●x150
Used engine ●x250
Reconditioned gearbox ●x395
Brake caliper ●x90
Brake drum ●x15
Brake disc (standard) ●x9
Brake disc (Cooper) ●x23
Brake pads ●x9
Brake shoes ●x10
Wheel bearing front or rear ●x16

Wing front (genuine) ●x52
Wing front (Clubman) ●x85
Wing front (pattern) ●x34
Subframe (genuine) ●x220
Subframe (pattern) ●x130
Radius arm (exchange) ●x35
Suspension cone (front or rear) ●x35
Shock absorbers (full set of 4) ●x50
Recon steering rack ●x30
Replacement shell ●x3600
Complete professional car restoration
    ●x6000
Full professional respray ●x2000

Parts that are hard to find
Trim bits for older cars can take time to locate if you need a totally factory fresh
restoration, as can some mechanical parts for the very early models.

Parts that are expensive
Most bits are very cheap, although the cost of repair panels needed to restore some
cars can mount up.

Genuine subframes can be expensive.

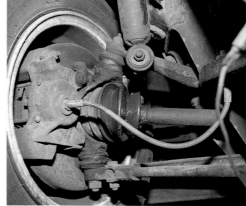

The rest of the running gear is cheap and
widely available.

3 Living with a Mini
– will you get along together?

The Mini was designed when the Suez crisis was causing major concern about the price and future availability of fuel, so small and economical had been the order of the day. Those attributes are still very relevant today; in fact, probably even more so, as the fuel and congestion situation has worsened to a level unimaginable in the 1950s. That the car ended up dynamic and potent, can be attributed to the design team, but even it couldn't have imagined that the little Mini would have such a long-lived appeal or been universally accepted as a motoring

The cars can be as luxurious or as Spartan as the owner wants.

milestone. But what is it really like to have a living legend on your driveway today?

Slip behind the wheel and the dynamism that ensured sales success is immediately apparent. The engine is willing to rev and provides an eager response to a firm right foot, and the car will run tight, flat and true through the sharpest of bends. It's a liberating vehicle to drive that provides thrills far beyond its humble specifications.

The reality of day-to-day living with a Mini, though, is not quite as simple as these first driving impressions would suggest. Early cars are noisy inside, with the engine sounding thrashed and uncomfortable as you press on, and the racket can be accompanied by levels of vibration which could shock someone used to more modern cars. The low seating position combined with what is really rather rudimentary suspension – compared to today's computer-designed smoothies – can be uncomfortable, particularly on bumpy, potholed roads, where your internal organs can feel like they're uncontrollably bouncing off each other. Chuck in an unsubtle graduation between power on and off, and the car can lurch uncomfortably if treated carelessly. Handling can also drift into understeer quite readily, although the inherent good design of the chassis means that simply backing off on the throttle restores equilibrium.

Early cars are the most challenging to use now as power output is rather modest for some of today's hurly-burly motoring, and the magic wand gear lever doesn't encourage quick changes. The lack of synchromesh on 1st can be a pain, as can the rather thinly-padded seats which do little to alleviate the bumpy ride. The cars are, however, the most charming, and capture the real spirit of the original Mini, which was a beguiling mixture of austerity and classy engineering. If your chosen car is not to be a daily runaround, then these Mark 1s are worth the effort, as long as your budget will stretch to it.

Cars from the late '60s through to the late '80s make perfectly acceptable choices for regular use. Performance levels increased, as did soundproofing, comfort and effectiveness of the brakes, without losing that essential cheeky charm. The last run of cars through the '90s were very well trimmed and, with the exception of the still jiggly ride, offered pretty modern motoring.

With the classic Mini now out of production, any model you choose is likely to be older than many less charismatic cars that have already been consigned to the scrapyard. This will inevitably mean that a higher level of maintenance is required compared to something more modern, as much through age and deterioration as the limitations imposed by the original design. The Mini offers the enthusiast a great opportunity to get his or her hands dirty; weekend tinkering is as much part of the ownership experience as time spent behind the wheel. If that prospect doesn't set your heart aflutter, then the Mini has an enormous number of dedicated specialists throughout the UK

The Mini has active clubs all around the world, with plenty of events to enjoy.

and overseas, although the humble local garage should not be overlooked either, as many of the mechanics lurking within will have cut their spannering teeth on this once ubiquitous little car.

With its appeal unlikely to wane the Mini is in the rare position of offering low ownership costs combined with a depreciation busting future if the battle against its Achilles heel (corrosion) is kept up, so it's always easier to buy the best car you can for your budget rather than restore (uneconomic on all but the most valuable models).

Despite its shortcomings, there are very few other cars out there that can offer the same pleasure levels as a Mini for a similar outlay. Even after a grim day at work, it's hard to keep the smile off your face once in the driver's seat. What more could you ask?

A Mini Van is cheap to run, easy to park, and a great advertising vehicle.

This chapter will attempt to give an idea, expressed as a percentage, of the relative value of individual models in good, useable condition. A concours car will be worth considerably more, and here the value gap between ages definitely narrows. A basket case would be around a tenth of the cost of a car in good condition, and perhaps even less. It's also important to bear in mind that fashions and demand change; for example, with each passing year the value of very late cars will drop and that of the rarer variants increase, so it's always worth checking the price guides in the classic car magazines to see if the model you're after is subject to any recent changes.

Coopers 1961-71 (100%)

Coopers are probably the ultimate expression of the sporting nature inherent in all Minis. The Mark 1 1275S is probably the most valuable, closely followed by the 1071S, with the 997s and 998s bringing up the rear. If you want a Cooper, join the Register, and make sure you're fully satisfied that all of the correct specifications are present before parting with your cash; there are a few misrepresented vehicles out there.

A 1275 S Cooper is highly desirable and has a price tag to match.

Rover Cabriolet (80% to 90%)

A small production run combined with an often pampered life means these cars are an attractive buy, so will carry a price tag to match. There are not that many out there, so you may have to travel to find the right car. Once you find it, though, all the usual Mini magic awaits, plus there's the benefit of 'wind in the hair' motoring.

Exterior hinge cars can command good prices, depending on their age and specification.

Early Minis – 1959 (75%)

The very earliest cars had some detail differences compared to the bulk of production. Assuming these rare bits are all present, these Minis will probably remain the most sought-after standard Saloon.

Their rarity and almost museum piece status means that few come up for sale, and are unlikely to be of interest to the mainstream enthusiast, instead remaining the preserve of the well-heeled collector.

Pick-ups (75%)
These are amazingly cute little commercials, and demand outstrips supply by some margin so prices are high. Many are modified, which distorts values in both directions depending on the desirability of the changes.

Mark 1 Mini – to 1967 (60%)
Once again rarity and purity of design keeps demand, and hence price, relatively high for early cars. They definitely have a charm of their own but must be kept as close to original as possible to make the top money. Not a car to buy if you want to stamp your own personality on something.

Vans (60%)
Although it wasn't the most popular commercial during its production lifespan these have shot up in value, with scarcity again having an impact on value. The very earliest flat roof versions will carry the biggest price tag. Still a versatile vehicle on today's congested city streets.

Vans are very popular and will always be worth more than Saloons from the same period, Pick-ups are even more highly-valued.

1990s cars (50%)
Worth decent money simply because they're still relatively recent, often with low mileage, dealer service history, etc. They are also the easiest to live with and come highly specified. The last models down the production line will become 100% in the near future as long as they have all

It's still possible to find a low mileage, good condition, unmolested car from the '90s.

the relevant paperwork and certificates. Don't be too easily seduced, however, as they can and do rot just as much as earlier cars.

1275 GT 1973-80 (40%)
An underrated Mini which was always considered the poor relation of the sporting cars which preceded it. This attitude is slowly changing and they will probably increase in value. In the meantime, they're a fun car to own and drive.

1970s cars (35%)
Little different from the more common eighties cars, but rarity and some very period paint hues boost their appeal.

Clubman (35%)
The squared-off front brought few admirers at the time, and in some Continental markets it was dropped very quickly. Estates are very common and are useful classic load haulers, although they may have had a hard life. Once again, period charm will have an influence on prices, which may rise.

1980s cars (25%)
Plentiful; and as a result values are lower. There are many special editions out there, but most have no impact on price. The ones that do will have something other than stickers and a paint job to justify the price gap, which could be up to 15% in the case of the 1100 Special, for example.

1970s Saloons have a definite retro charm.

The Clubman has a growing following, its relative rarity keeping prices up.

1980s Saloons are pretty much at the bottom of the desirability pile.

5 Before you view
– be well informed

Once you've found a car that may be of interest, it might be worthwhile to consider some, or all, of the following points. Doing so will help you decide whether or not a particular vehicle is worth pursuing.

Where is the car?
The days of your local paper having dozens of Minis in its classifieds are sadly long gone, but there should still be several on offer within a reasonable distance. However, if you're after something a little out of the ordinary, then you'll most definitely have to budget time and money to go and view the car you want.

Cost of collection and delivery
If you're buying a roadworthy legal Mini, then you can simply drive it home after ensuring that you have arranged appropriate insurance. If you've bought a restoration project, then costs will rapidly mount if you have to rely on someone else to move it for you. Always try to get a quote for this before you view your prospective purchase, and incorporate the cost into your negotiations.

Dealer or private sale?
Minis are pretty much the preserve of specialists now, although they do appear in classic car dealers' showrooms. Dealer prices will have been set to include overheads, guarantees and advertising, but at least you'll have some comeback if anything goes wrong. If buying privately, make sure you see the car at the address on the V5 (ownership papers) and avoid anyone who only uses a mobile phone and offers to bring the car to you, or wants to meet at a car park or petrol station.

Reason for sale?
If the car is being sold by a specialist, then the answer is quite simple; it's their living. Private vendors, though, may have a much wider range of reasons, most of which are perfectly valid, but always ask the question; it still takes some people by surprise, and the hurried answer that you receive might raise some doubts.

When and where?
Always view a car in daylight, and preferably not when it's raining, as a damp sheen can make even the worst paintwork look half decent; as does fading light. Once again, it's worth making sure that the viewing address matches that on the ownership papers.

Condition
Before you view, ask the seller for an honest appraisal of the vehicle's condition, tell them you're coming from some distance away, which usually helps, as they're likely to at least own up to the blatantly obvious defects. If it doesn't sound very promising there are plenty of other Minis out there, so don't waste your time needlessly.

All original specification?
The Mini has always attracted a lot of individual modifications, the desirability of

which is very much down to the prospective owner. Bog standard specifications and factory colours still rule the roost, though, as they tend to fetch higher prices and are easier to re-sell if need be; shocking pink might be your favourite colour, but it might limit the car's appeal to future buyers.

Matching numbers?
Minis have a chassis plate riveted to the bonnet slam panel. There may also be one or two other plates, commission and car numbers mounted here depending on model and year, and later cars also had a plate mounted on the inner wing. The engine number is stamped on the block and is easy to spot, although you may have to wipe away some oily sludge to read it, so the vendor should be able to confirm that the numbers match the paperwork before you arrive, but double-check them yourself. Altering identities is pretty simple with cars of this age, so if you're looking at a high value variant make sure that you do your homework on the correct fixtures and fittings.

Is the seller the legal owner?
In the UK the ownership papers record the registered keeper of the vehicle which may not be the actual owner. Ask the vendor if they are the legal owner, and if not, get some contact details of the person who is and check that they're aware that the car is being sold.

Is the vehicle taxed and tested?
All countries have some sort of roadworthiness check – in the UK this is referred to as the MoT. Inspect the certificate to see how long it's valid for, and make sure the registration and chassis numbers match the car you're looking at. Don't rely on the presence of a valid certificate as a guarantee of the car's condition, though; it merely reflects the state of many components at the time of testing and in the opinion of the person doing the examination. There are a few comebacks if the test has been incorrectly carried out or if it is suspected of being illegally obtained, but it's better to check the vehicle thoroughly yourself and avoid heartache later. In the UK, road tax for Minis is in one of the lower brackets, although that may change as older cars are demonised for their emissions, and any made before 1973 are currently exempt. Other countries have similar concessions for older vehicles.

Unleaded conversion?
Minis built before October 1988 cannot use unleaded fuel, so either require the use of a fuel additive, or the head can be swapped for a compatible one at reasonable cost which will soon be recouped. Cars fitted with a catalytic converter can use unleaded petrol only.

How can you pay?
There's no doubt that a wad of cash can be a useful lever to get the price down when you're negotiating. If you're unsure about carrying a large amount around with you, a personal cheque could be left, although collection would probably have to wait until it had cleared, or you could use a banker's draft drawn on your account in the vendor's name. Many sellers are now wary of these, however, as fraudulent versions are not uncommon. Dealers are usually the most flexible when it comes to payment methods, and will normally accept credit and debit cards.

Are you insured to drive if you buy?

There are several ways to cover yourself to drive home in your newly purchased Mini, many using a policy initially arranged for other vehicles. This may be attractive in the short term as it can save money, but should there be an accident, the amount of cover provided would probably not cover the value of the car. Classic policies are cheap and not necessarily that restrictive if you shop around, so make sure you're adequately insured before hitting the highway.

Professional vehicle checks

Many motoring organisations around the world offer this type of service for their members, and they should have no trouble examining a Mini, although it might be better to get a specialist to do it for you, as the cost may be less and they should be well used to all the car's idiosyncrasies. Whoever does it, make sure they have liability insurance so you can make a claim in case they miss anything which proves to be expensive later.

Data checks

Once again, national motoring organisations can help find out the history of your car; whether it has been stolen, written off, or is subject to an outstanding hire purchase agreement, for example. In the UK the best known organisation is HPI (01722 422 422). HPI provides a compensation scheme in case any of the information supplied is inaccurate.

6 Inspection equipment
– these items will really help

This book
The major defects that you're likely to find in any prospective purchase are outlined in this book. It would be all too easy to forget important checks in the excitement of viewing a new car, but if you keep this volume to hand and work your way through the sections methodically using the unique marking system, it will help make up your mind and could save a lot of your hard-earned money from being wasted.

Magnet
Take a weak one, if it's too strong it will cling on through the layers of filler that you're hoping to discover. When you do use it, don't scrape it along the paintwork, but rather apply and remove it with care; remember that the car you're looking at is someone else's pride and joy until you stump up the cash to make it yours.

Overalls
Sadly, Minis rust, which means you'll have to roll about on the ground to find out the extent of the rot. A set of overalls can be discarded after the inspection, so you can take a test drive without sullying the car interior and irritating the seller.

Torch
There are lots of nooks and crannies in a Mini's body, and a torch will make both under-bonnet and under-body inspection easier, even on the brightest of days.

Spectacles (if you need them for close work)
Most cars will have had some filler in them at some time, and unless it's been applied with care, there will be small telltale marks under the paint, so take your specs if you need them for close up work, as a detailed look at some areas will be needed.

Jack and axle stands
Minis are very low cars, and it may be sensible to use a jack to get some additional height to allow a clearer view. Always use axle stands, having first made sure that the ground is level and firm enough to support the car safely.

Having found a possible purchase, asked all the necessary questions over the phone, and assembled your inspection equipment, you should now find yourself confronting a Mini in the metal. The most important thing is to make sure that your heart doesn't rule your head, so keep calm by thinking about how long it has taken to save up the money. It should be possible to eliminate obvious heaps very quickly, hence this 15 minute examination, by the end of which you'll know if the car warrants further time and effort.

Exterior

First impressions count, but don't fall for shiny paintwork. Look instead at how the car sits; hydrolastic-suspended cars may be lopsided or low all round, and even those relying on rubber cones can sag thanks to worn bushes on the suspension or damaged arm pivots. Continue the general assessment by looking down the length of the car, tilting your head until the light catches the panels which will then throw poorly filled areas or dents into sharp relief. Concentrate on the door bottoms, the sides low down between the back of the door opening and the wheelarch, and the A-panels in front of the doors, in particular. Check the body seams for blistering corrosion and then move up to the roof and guttering for more of the same. The area around the front and rear screens may have flaking, bubbling or scabby paint, and the box section above the doors also rusts and develops holes. At the front of the car, inspect the wings, especially where they meet the front panel, the bonnet, and the scuttle. Cheap replacement panels are often a poor fit which will require a fair degree of skill and time to make them line up correctly. If the metalwork looks new, has it received enough care to ensure that the bonnet gaps are even? Is there any

The large flat panels on the sides will reveal defects if you allow the light to cut across them.

Look for bubbling that indicates problems below the surface.

sign of seam sealer having been used to make up for deficiencies in the panels?

Look behind each front wheel, inside the arch, at the bulkhead and the front end of the sills (rocker panels), both of which suffer from road debris. If this area has been repaired previously, has it been done neatly? Make sure that the tyres are

The top of the B-posts rot, though filler may hide the true extent of the rust.

The whole front end corrodes badly. This example has lost its seams as they have been filled.

Door misalignment spells trouble; is it hinge wear or worse?

evenly worn, if not the tracking may be out, or there may be wear in the rack, track rod ends, or suspension bushes. Open and shut each door in turn; any sign of them lifting up and onto their strikers as they close, or dropping as they open, is potentially a big problem and will require further investigation if you think the car warrants it. Look at the top of the doorstep, which often corrodes. Is it still in the original paint or has it been undersealed? Check the sills; a quick glance will do at the moment, and will tell you if they've been patched or blacked out with more underseal. Are there sill trim strips in place? If so, do they fit well or is corrosion or poorly welded repairs pushing them off? At the back end check the boot (trunk) lid for signs of rust, particularly at the bottom, and then see if the panel it hinges on is rotten at the seam where it meets the rear valence; it usually is, and this seemingly innocuous corrosion can indicate expensive problems ahead. The valence itself may be rusty and split at the bottom. Open the boot and lift the covering if one is fitted, and check for holes in the corners, left and right. Finally, get on your knees, stick your head under the

back end and have a quick look at the rear subframe. If there is obvious rust, signs of repair plates on the bottom, or suspiciously large amounts of new underseal, then assume that it's shot and will need replacement, which is expensive and nearly always leads to more work, either to the body or the mechanical items attached to the frame itself. Whilst there, look at the tyres for signs of irregular wear, which could mean that the radius arm bearings are on the way out.

Interior

Fortunately, the Mini is so basic inside that its defects are easy to spot. The seats often sag, the covers are not particularly robust so split easily, and even the frames come apart at the seams. The door trims are card covered in vinyl, and they warp and split from a combination of age and damp, problems which the carpets also suffer from; and wet carpets mean rusty floors. The instrument panel is simple, even on the best-equipped versions, but check for any additional holes left by a previous owner's attempts to 'upgrade.' Have a look at the headlining whilst you're in there as it's tricky and expensive to replace.

All materials used for Mini seats are prone to splitting.

Mechanicals

The engine bay is unlikely to be pristine unless you're viewing a recently restored car, but it shouldn't be an oil congealed, dirty mess either, as that's an indication of a general lack of care. Pull out the dipstick and check the oil level; it should be near the top mark and the lubricant should not be black and thin. Wipe a little on the end of your finger and roll it around for a second to see if it feels gritty, and then smell it; very cheap stuff can give off a faint aroma of ammonia, old oil can smell burnt. Neither is good, particularly as the gearbox relies on it for lubrication as well. Check for signs of a creamy-brown emulsion on the stick which would indicate head gasket problems. Take off the radiator cap and check the state of the coolant, it should be clean and brightly coloured depending on the type of anti-freeze, you don't want to see scummy, orange rusty water, or a creamy emulsion like you checked for on the dipstick, which again would indicate a head problem.

Position yourself where you can clearly see the exhaust tail pipe and ask the vendor to start the engine. The motor should fire up promptly from cold (and if the car was hot when you arrived ask why) and it's common for combustion to be accompanied by a short puff of smoke as the small amount of oil that has crept past worn valve

The condition of the oil can tell you a lot about the likely state of the engine.

stem oil seals burns off. The important thing here is that the smoke should clear very quickly indeed. If the car continues to produce a blue haze after more than a few seconds, then there's piston or ring wear, particularly likely if the amount of smoke increases with engine speed. Black smoke when the engine is revved in short bursts means that the mixture is too rich, and white or grey smoke indicates the presence of water, which may clear once the car is warm (if it doesn't, then the head gasket is once again the primary suspect).

While you have the bonnet (hood) up, ask the seller to rock the steering wheel from side-to-side as you look at the top mountings for the front subframe (these are large-headed sleeve bolts on later cars – 1976-on; earlier cars were solidly mounted to the shell). As the steering moves there should be no visible movement at the bushes. In really bad cases the whole frame may be seen moving in time with the steering wheel. Replacing the mounts is a tedious and potentially awkward job so check carefully.

Finish off your fifteen minutes listening to the engine. Does it idle evenly and quietly? Are there any knocks and rattles? Are the tappets clattering? If they are it could either be a sign of poor maintenance or a dry top end which indicates oiling problems or irregular changes of lubricant. Does it look standard under there or have things been altered; if so why? Are there any signs of coolant leaks? Does the gearbox chatter at idle, and if so, how noisy is it? A gearbox change is a major outlay, and if the noise is loud enough to attract attention it probably spells trouble.

Is it worth staying for a longer look?

The answer, of course, depends on the amount being asked for the car and the level of expectation attached to that price tag. If you're looking to do a complete restoration none of the above may be a problem, although it's best to avoid cars with gutter and extensive seam corrosion unless you're confident of your abilities with a welder on thin panels. If the car is being sold at around the market price for that model in good condition, then finding subframe problems or dropped doors may be much more of an issue. If things seem OK so far, or at least not so bad that you've been put off, then it's time to move on to a far more searching and critical examination; so get out the overalls, you're going to get dirty!

8 Key points
– where to look for problems

Rear subframes are expensive to buy in either genuine or aftermarket form, and the work involved in replacing them is considerable as the corrosion will almost certainly have spread into the back of the shell, which will have to be repaired before a new frame is fitted. Brake pipes, battery leads, handbrake cables, and radius arms may all need attention at the same time.

The sill structure is unusual on a Mini, but it plays a vital part in keeping the car strong. Poor repairs can and do seriously weaken the whole car, particularly if cover panels have been used over old rusty metal. This is an area that demands a thorough investigation, as sorting out bodged repairs will be time-consuming.

Problems with the boot floor may have spread further than imagined. The rear is attached to the hinge panel and valence and can be tricky to sort out. Any corrosion in the left-hand corner will mean tank removal before any repairs can be carried out. The section where the subframe mounts may also be holed, so repair panels will have to be accurately placed to ensure everything lines up again.

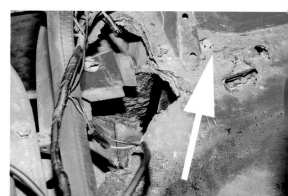

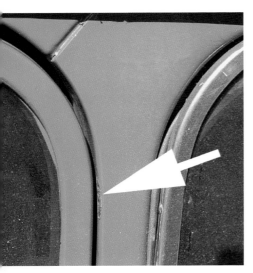

Dropped doors can mean major structural work to the A-post area. Even an innocuous mark on the B-post, like the one pictured, should be regarded with deep suspicion; this was caused by a weak hinge panel allowing the door to contact the post as it shut.

The radius arms wear and, although straightforward to replace if exchange ones are purchased, there's always the possibility of pin seizure which can throw a spanner in the works. The metalwork surrounding this area also has to be in perfect condition, as the subframe stresses are fed into the shell here.

Score each section as follows: 4 = excellent; 3 = good, 2 = average; 1 = poor

Exterior

Paintwork

In the 15 minute examination shiny paint was deliberately ignored to concentrate on more gritty issues, but now is the time to assess just how good the paintwork really is. If the car has been resprayed very recently it may well have been done to cover up lots of bodged repairs so the owner can shift the car at a healthy profit. Look for signs of a rushed job; for example, overspray on the window rubbers and door seals, or an orange peel finish, or dull, flat sections where there's an inadequate depth of paint. If the finish looks original and carries normal battle scars and dents it may well have faded, and if the surface has gone 'milky' it could be beyond saving, no matter how much time and T-Cut you lavish on it. With resprays now costing very large sums of money it could be a budget buster if you need your Mini to be shiny.

Front panels

The whole of the front end must be re-examined more critically than during the 15 minute inspection. The wings blister and hole around the headlamps thanks to the poultice of road muck that lodges behind them, and the joint with the front panel also suffers. The backs of the wings rot out by the scuttle and down the trailing edge next to the seam. Hopefully the days of blatant bodges are over, thanks to tighter annual testing procedures, but just in case, make sure that if the wings have been replaced that they're securely welded on; rivets or self-

The wing-to-front panel area is a prime spot for rust.

tapping screws are not acceptable. Pop your head in the wheelarch and check the area around the shock absorber mountings on the inner wings. While you're in there

have another prod around the front end of the sills and bulkhead and look for previous repairs. Even the bonnet is not immune, with the leading edge blistering

The back of the wings are often filled.

Look under the bumper, too; you could be in for a surprise ...

Check around the mounting plate for the front shocks.

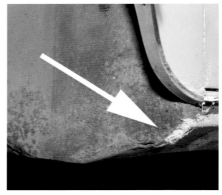

This area suffers from the effects of road debris thrown up by the wheel.

The front of the bonnet rots, as do the rear corners.

The inner wing can hole along its entire length.

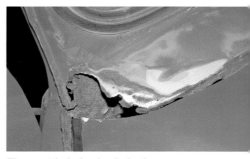

The scuttle holes badly in the corners, so check for filled repairs.

and holing above the trim and at the rear corners. Make sure that it sits squarely, with even gaps all around, then open it and check the inner wings on both sides. Look for signs of distortion that may indicate accident damage, as well as corrosion. The upper bulkhead can rust, especially around the fuse box, but may be covered by sound deadening material.

This closing plate rots away, as does the area around the fresh air vents.

Check the scuttle area, a prime area for a spot of bodging, making sure that the panel gaps are good (or even that they exist; they are often filled right over). Underneath, there's a closing plate which rots out, and there may be corrosion around the fresh air vent holes immediately under that (where fitted). Try and get your hand up under the scuttle from inside the wheelarch and feel if the closing plate is still there; be careful, though, as there may be sharp, rusty edges waiting to cut you. Re-check around the screen looking for filler, especially in the lower corners.

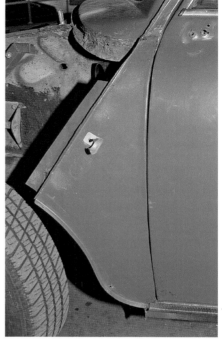

Blistering here spells trouble for the hinge panel behind.

The last parts on the front end to inspect are the A-panels, which rot mainly at the bottom and next to the seam, though on bad cars rot can erupt just about anywhere. These panels are cheap to buy and simple to fit but can cover up rust damage to the hinge panel underneath, which is trickier to sort out, especially on cars with external hinges. If you find signs of rot, exercise additional care when checking the doors later. Make sure that the join to the front wing has not split at the bottom.

Clubman front end

The Clubman front panels are of a different design, but rust attacks them just as vigorously. Check the wings where they meet the adjoining panels, and especially where the inner, outer and slam panels converge. The leading edge rusts thanks to trapped mud, as does the metal surrounding the headlight. The front panel (upper and lower) can rot just about anywhere. The subframe mounts on a pair of bent metal brackets attached to the lower front

Clubman wings corrode just as badly as those on round-nosed cars.

Clubman bonnets hole at the front.

panel, and these must be completely sound, as must the metal they're welded to. The inner wings rust, as does the leading edge of the bonnet. All in all, the Clubman is just as bad as the round-nosed Mini, but replacement parts are far more expensive, which encourages temporary repairs rather than correct rectification work.

Front subframe   4 3 2 1

The front subframe, unlike the rear, is not particularly rust-prone, mainly due to the amount of oil that A-series engines manage to leak out onto it. This doesn't mean that it should be ignored, though, so check the front bar in particular for signs of damage or creasing.

Middle section panels   4 3 2 1

Starting at the top check the guttering once more and the edges of the roof. If the car has a vinyl roof, whether factory-fitted like the Special or aftermarket, make sure that it's securely attached, and be suspicious of any irregularities underneath. Open the doors in turn and try to move them up and down when nearly fully extended. There will probably be some movement so try to track down its source. Start by watching the hinges, but if there's still relative movement to the shell once the slack is taken up then the mounting panel is rotten, and it may even be possible to see the whole pillar flexing. The doors rust along the bottom and are often filled, so look for signs of bubbling under the paint. The outer skin can split at the top regardless of whether wind-up or sliding windows are fitted. The inner frame corrodes at the bottom

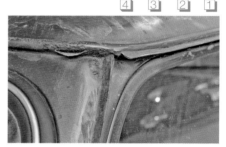

Guttering can be crusty and, if the rot has spread into the roof panel, will need skilled repair.

Weak hinges and welded doors spell trouble.

Door bottoms rot from the inside out.

The door frame can split at the glass aperture.

The step panel is often holed; be suspicious of underseal.

Inner sills rust, so check these carefully, especially around seatbelt mountings.

Previous repairs may simply have been slapped over old rust.

thanks to blocked drain holes, as does the wrap-over of the outer skin. Check the glass frames where they meet the main body of the door as they regularly crack at this point.

The doorstep suffers badly so expect holes, particularly at the curved ends where the step meets the A- and B-posts. The outer sill-to-step joint trim may be bulging and loose thanks to underlying rot forcing it away from the steel; the same situation can be caused by lumpy welding when a new step or sill is fitted. The sill itself can be rotten just about anywhere, but especially at the front and back near the wheelarch. Check whether it's an original panel or whether it has been replaced before; non-genuine replacements are much

This floor has been creased by a carelessly placed jack.

deeper, often lack the correct drainage pressings, and will usually be stitch welded in place rather than spot welded. Lots of seam sealer and underseal indicate a bodged job. Put a finger in the jacking point to check that it's still in one piece inside the sill, as it often rots away and isn't repaired before a new outer is welded in place.

Inside the car the inner sills should be checked for rot along their entire length. Repairs may be fine if done well, but many aren't, so look for crude patches secured by lumpy irregular welds, if they've suffered this fate it will all need doing again very soon. When the car was built the inner sill was made as a single pressing with the floorpan, which makes it easy to see if a section has been welded in, the other giveaway is that the repair panels are made to stop at the seat box, whereas the original continues uninterrupted underneath it. Once again, correct repairs are fine, but many are just slapped on over old rust, and a combination of poor welding inside the car and oversize outer sills can seriously weaken the shell, as the stress points are no longer as the designer intended. The front inner arches and bulkhead are rot prone, including the join of the dash to the bulkhead.

Floorpans rust quite readily, with the corner at the bulkhead and inner arch being the favoured starting point, although it may be present mid-floor, too. If the car you're inspecting has had its carpets glued down assume the worst. There may be a heavy bitumen-like coating on the floor of later cars which can disguise their true state. Treat any cracks with suspicion, and try to pick some of the covering away with a small screwdriver to see what lies underneath. There's a box section running under the floor carrying the battery cable to the engine compartment, and corrosion directly above this is very common. The front subframe mounts are on the toe board; find them and prod the surrounding metal to make sure that it's completely sound, and that there are no signs of distorted metal which would indicate accident damage.

The rear floorpan rots like the front, so look in the corners next to the storage

Floors can rot above the box section on the underside.

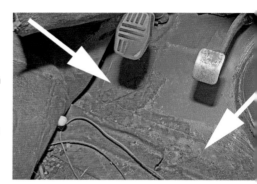

Check the floor where it meets the toe board for rot and accident damage.

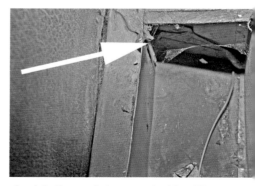

Look in the pockets on each side of the back seat, as the subframe mounts here.

boxes, and inside them, too. Remove the cardboard liner, which should flex to allow it to be pulled free, then use a torch to check the bottoms for rust. At the back of the box are the subframe mounts, so check for rust or the indications of its imminent arrival, such as discoloured paint and blistering steel. Between the boxes is the main part of the panel, and this will also show signs of rust damage on some cars. If you find any, then the whole section will have to be replaced when the subframe is out (expensive). Have a look at the metal under the side windows and rear screen whilst you're in there, as they can rust around the apertures.

Rear end panels

Check the back wings for damage and corrosion at the bottom on each side of the wheelarch and also under the back windows. Have a long hard look at the back of the sill and the adjacent metalwork where the rear subframe mounts; you don't want to see scabs, badly welded repair patches, or lots of underseal. On bad but original cars it may be possible to see distortion in the metal due to rust-weakened mounts. Try pushing the back of the car down and looking for movement between the shell and the subframe. Make sure that the closing plates visible at the back of the arch are sound. Check the back panel around the filler neck and under the rear lights for rust, then move in to the boot. Inspect the edges for previous repairs, whether rust or accident induced, and

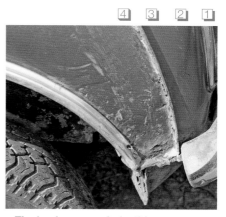

The back corners hole; this one was a mess so the repair was easily spotted.

The back panel suffers, too. Three sections are welded together and this one has lost two through corrosion.

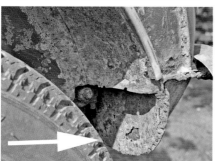

These small closing plates are actually structural so must be in good condition.

Boot floors rot and may also be impact damaged.

attempts to disguise it, often including filler.

The rust can extend several inches into the boot, and even attack the spare wheel well, so pull out the rim and have a look. The battery should still have its cover plate in place; check around the edge of its compartment for signs of it separating from the boot floor. The left-hand suspension tower will be out of sight thanks to the petrol tank (or both sides if you're looking at a Cooper S) but the other will be visible and may be rusty to the point of holing; if it is then the hidden one will be just as bad. Double-check from outside, although it can be hard to spot as the shock absorbers are in the way and the area may be undersealed. Have a glance at the seam where the inner wing and boot floor joins whilst you're under there as it can swell and split.

Estate, Van and Pick-up rear end

These versions rust along the bottom seam between the doors and the back end, and seem to suffer from rotten inner wheelarches even more frequently than Saloons. Petrol tanks are in an exposed position on most models (very early Estates had them mounted inside), at the rear underside, and they do rust out, so check for leaks. Window frames rot, as does the metal underneath, which can be tricky to repair. Back doors split

The rear window frames trap water and rust out the metal underneath.

and corrode at the bottom, in particular, and around the bottom hinges on the body side. The rear pillars break away from the back panel and floor which can allow the whole aperture to flex, so check them for signs of movement during the test drive.

Pick-up and Van load bays will have had a hard life, so will often be dented as

Van and Estate rear doors corrode at the bottom, around the glass, and on the skin above the pressings on the underside.

The corners of the shell at the back door openings can split.

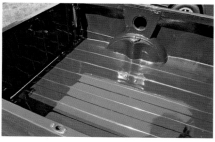

Van and Pick-up load bays are often dented from years of hard work, so it will be difficult finding one this good.

The wood on Estate versions isn't structural, but is still expensive to sort out if rotten.

well as rusty, which is expensive to put right if you must have a commercial in perfect condition. Check that the floor is still attached all the way round its edge. Early Estates were available with wood trim at the rear, which is not structural like the Morris Minor; these are simply glued onto the metal. They do swell and rot, though, and will dent your budget severely to replace, so check every inch for discoloured or soft patches, and look for signs of sealant or filler used to disguise their condition.

Cabriolet

⁴ ³ ² ¹

Convertible Minis have been made by several concerns over the years, notably by Crayford and Lamm, but the most common is the late Rover version. All the above checks are relevant (excluding gutter rot, obviously) to which should be added the extra strengtheners inside the car, which are along the inner sill, the seat box, the rear seat pan, and the A-panels. Check that all the additional trim is present and in good condition, and that the small rear windows wind up and down correctly. Make sure that the hood opens and closes without a struggle, and that the frame isn't rusty or twisted. The fabric should be examined for nicks and tears as replacements are expensive. There should be a colour co-ordinated bag to store it in when folded. The body kit is also the largest fitted to a Mini and so is prone to knocks. Once again, replacement parts aren't cheap, and, as they're finished in metallic paint, even scratches can be wallet-busting to sort out.

Rear subframe

⁴ ³ ² ¹

Probably the best known defect in the Mini's design, the rear frame rusts badly all over. The flat bottom plates can be clearly seen, and your 15 minute inspection should have given you a rough idea of their condition. Check once again that

Battery boxes split and rust because they're in an exposed position.

they've not been repaired before, and then have a look at the side webbing where possible; any crustiness spells trouble. The front end of the frame traps mud and dirt against the body and rots that out too. Check the condition of the underside of the battery box whilst in the area, as it's often rusty around the seams, to the point of holing.

Exterior trim

4️⃣ 3️⃣ 2️⃣ 1️⃣

Check the grille for damage as they're surprisingly expensive for pre-1970 cars. Chrome bumpers rust, although stainless items are an option; check their security, too, especially the rear, as the mounting bolts are often sheared/missing. Door and boot handles blister and disfigure, but replacements aren't too expensive. Make sure that they all work during your inspection, including the locking filler cap, if fitted. Door mirrors can be wobbly and chrome ones rust. Wheelarch trim and body kits cannot be repaired easily, and replacements increased in cost as sizes got bigger.

Grille damage is purely cosmetic, but they're not cheap to replace on some versions.

Bumpers rust but are fairly cheap to replace.

Wipers

Make sure that the wipers are fully operational as the metal spiral that drives them can be prone to seizure. Check, too, for excessive slop in the spindles, which allows the blades to come into contact with the screen rubber.

Wiper mechanisms become sloppy, and end up clearing part of the scuttle rather than the glass.

Glass/rubbers

The screen should be free of damage or scratch marks in the swept area, or it will be a roadworthiness test failure in many countries. The screen rubber can perish, as can the chromed plastic insert that yellows and becomes brittle over time. If rear pop-outs are fitted, make sure that they open and lock in place.

Glass seals rot and the chromed insert loses its lustre over time.

If the car has pop-out rear glass, make sure the mechanism still locks.

Lights

Most Minis have sealed beam headlights, although many will have been replaced

or upgraded to versions with replaceable bulbs, or even halogen units. Check the state of the reflectors to make sure that the silvering is not damaged. Headlights, front indicators and wing repeaters, where fitted, are potentially troublesome, thanks to their exposed positions, allowing damp and corrosion to interfere with correct operation.

Wheels and tyres

Many Minis will have had their standard wheels replaced with alloys. Check these carefully for signs of impact, as even slight damage which can simply be knocked out on a steel rim may mean the scrap pile for an alloy. If the car has been a factory special edition fitted with alloys, finding

Headlights lose their silvering.

the correct replacement may prove difficult. Tyres should be checked for sidewall damage or signs of irregular wear.

Interior

Seats

Mini seats split, fade and sag. Fronts are often replaced with racier aftermarket versions, which are fine, but if you want to maintain originality then it's either a hunt for better secondhand ones, or choose from a restricted range of covers and rebuild your own.

Original seat covers split, fade or unravel, depending on type.

Lining

Headlining gets damaged and yellows with age. Replacements are available in a range of colours but they're not especially cheap, and replacing them is a tricky DIY job.

A dirty, insecure headlining like this could be expensive to replace.

Door trims

These can be bought off-the-shelf in a few colours, but anything else will need to be made, so check the ones on the car carefully for splits, sagging from damp, or gaping holes from past efforts at in-car entertainment.

Interior trim suffers from damp, and warps easily.

Mats/carpets

Check the carpets under the dash for dampness which may indicate a leaking heater matrix. Elsewhere, carpets may be damp from leaking door seals or holes in the floor. If they're worn out or shabby, a new set can be bought very cheaply from a Mini specialist.

Handles

Interior door handles and window

Handles break but are simple to replace.

winders snap, and the knobs fall off. The earliest doors had a pull string to release the lock – make sure that they're still in place, as many were changed over to short, chromed levers.

Steering wheels   4   3   2   1
Early wheels were large, hard plastic items, which wore well but eventually split between the indentations on the underside. Later wheels are padded (depending on specification) but still split or become sticky with age, which does little to enhance the driving experience. Aftermarket steering wheels are commonplace as a result. Whatever type is fitted, grasp it at the top and bottom and push and pull to check for wear in the steering column bushes.

Instruments   4   3   2   1
Early Minis and the cheaper versions of later cars had a speedometer set in the middle of the dash, with warning lights enclosed within. Controls were on flick switches underneath, which were a fair reach from the driving seat when wearing a seatbelt. Later and more upmarket cars have a 2, or 3, instrument binnacle in front of the driver, still enclosing the warning lights with a row of rocker switches in the centre. There are minor variations to this layout, with additional oil pressure gauges, ammeters and rev counters on some versions, plus a plethora of aftermarket kits for the proud owner to upgrade his or her Mini. Whatever is fitted make sure that it all works as it should. Erratic performance may be due to problems with the fuse box, which is easily replaced, or it may be down to old and 'crusty' wiring, which is more of a problem.

Instrumentation is basic on even the best-equipped Mini.

Make sure that all of the switches and controls function as they should.

Controls   4   3   2   1
Just like the instruments, check that the stalk-mounted controls work as they should; that's the indicators plus the telltale, main beam and its warning light, and the horn. Check that the pedal rubbers are in place and not too worn, or that can be a roadworthiness test failure.

Mechanics
The engine   4   3   2   1
During the 15 minute examination you will no doubt have seen how externally oily

Check that lubricant is getting to the top end.

Oil leaks abound; this one has clean patches at several crucial points, which indicates that the flow is fairly strong.

the engine was. Now you must try to assess where those leaks are coming from, as some are expensive to fix. The worst to sort out are the engine to gearbox seal, and the one between the diff housing and the gearbox. Oil from the bottom of the bellhousing cover means there's a leak behind the clutch. Driveshaft output seals wear, so give the inner joints a wiggle if it's wet under there; if they move about to any great degree then the bearings in the box are on the way out and changing seals will not make a difference. The gear change shaft seal fails regularly, but it's easy to swap. The area around the oil filter is often wet, but again isn't usually a problem, and the same goes for cars fitted with an external oil cooler, although the costs may rise here. The most common fault, and one which causes the most obvious mess, is a leaking rocker cover gasket, which is quick and easy to change.

Take off the oil filler cap and peer inside, the rocker shaft should be wet and oily, poorly-maintained cars will have a dry appearance, or may be black with a sticky sludge. Any sign of light brown sludge indicates a possible head gasket problem. Start the engine and listen to the top end which should have a smooth rhythmic chatter from the valve gear. If it's noisy or harsh then the tappets need to be adjusted or the rocker shaft is worn. Rev the engine gently and, as it backs off, listen for the tinkle of a worn timing chain, repeat the process but rev it a little harder, this time try to hear if there's a knock from the bottom of the engine as the load comes off which would indicate big end wear.

Gearbox

This should not be noisy at idle; if there's a chattering sound the bearings may be worn. If the sound seems concentrated at the bellhousing end, then the idler gear bearing may be damaged. Depress the clutch, if the noise disappears that will pretty much confirm the diagnosis. Check the clutch slave cylinder for leaks, and have a good look at the pushrod that transfers movement from it. If there are signs of anything having been welded to it then there are problems ahead as clutch clearance is lost on motors with bad crankshaft end float and then regained by

Slave cylinders leak: check, too, that the pushrod has not been extended.

bodging an extension onto the rod to compensate.

Automatic gearbox 4 3 2 1

The auto box in Minis is often criticised for being weak, but this reputation has more to do with owner neglect than any inherent defects. The box shares its oil with the engine, like the manual version, but, as it has many narrow passageways and valve blocks, it will not tolerate old, dirty lubricant, so re-do your dipstick check and ask the seller how often the oil is changed. Leaks from the torque converter housing can be expensive to rectify. Check that the inhibitor works and that the car will only start in park, then slip the box into drive. If it clunks noisily there may be wear in the engine mounts, or a defect in the gearbox which can be checked during the test drive.

Radiator and cooling system 4 3 2 1

Look for signs of leaks, damage, or rust staining to the radiator. Thermostat housing nuts seize and studs get broken during attempts to remove them, so make sure that they're all there. Water pumps aren't overly robust, so check the fanbelt for tension; if it's correct but there's still a high-pitched rhythmic squeaking from that area as the engine idles, the pump bearings are on the way out. Check for signs of water staining, particularly under the pump and around the small bypass hose. Make sure that the heater valve mounted on the left-hand side of the head is free to move, and that it's not leaking.

The coolant should be bright and colourful. Rusty, oily scum spells trouble.

Brakes 4 3 2 1

Check the brake master cylinder (and clutch while you're at it) for fluid level and signs of leakage, including inside the car. Check that the handbrake works properly, that it releases cleanly, and the ratchet is not worn (which can be tested by gently banging down on the lever when it's fully on). Brake backplates

Check the brakes for leaks and make sure that servos (if fitted) work correctly.

should be checked for fluid staining and damaged adjuster heads, calipers for signs of leakage.

Hubs, steering joints and rack

With the car jacked up grasp each front wheel in turn at the top and bottom (6 o'clock position) and try to rock it. If play is detected, it'll probably be due to worn ball joints. Turn the wheel to full lock to allow your head to peer round it, and double-check. There's also the possibility of wear in the arm mounts so look where the pin passes through for any hint of wobble. Whilst checking make sure there are signs of recent grease in the nipple next to the upper arm mount; it's frequently forgotten when servicing is carried out. If you suspect that wheel bearing wear may also be present, get someone to press the brake while you wiggle the rim, which will take bearing wear out of the equation until the brake is released once more. Give the wheel a spin and listen for any noise, although

Ball joints should be free of play, and the CV boots should have no splits or be leaking grease.

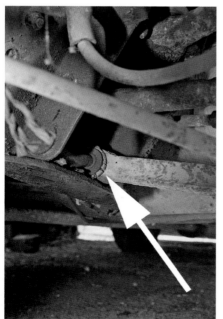

it may be difficult to get it turning fast enough to produce any. Move your hands to each side (9.15 position) of the rim and wiggle once more; this will show up play in the steering. Look for signs of movement in the rack or its mounts as replacement is time consuming. With the wheel still in the air and on full lock check the brake pipes for rust and the flexible hoses for splitting or leaks. Check the condition of the tie bars which stop the lower arm moving back and forth, they're often bent from ill advised

Check the bushes on all suspension components for cracking or other signs of deterioration.

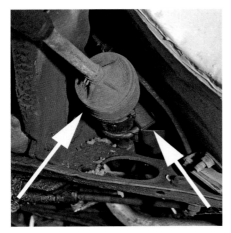

If the securing nut moves in time with the arm then the whole lot is seized internally which will wear the mounting hole in the subframe oval. Whilst there, check that the handbrake quadrants are free to pivot.

Radius arms should show signs of regular lubrication and have no play in relation to the side plates.

The rack mounting rubbers should be sound, and the boots in one piece and secure.

use of jacks; check their rubber bushes for splitting, too.

Radius arms

The radius arms wear due to inadequate lubrication so look for signs of a grease gun having been used recently. Grasp the wheel and try to pull it in and out, away from the subframe; there should be no signs of movement between the arm and the mounting plate. If there is, a new pin or reconditioned arm will be needed.

Battery and charging

Waggle the alternator or dynamo pulley for signs of bearing wear; once running they will rumble. Take a multimeter with you if you want to fully check the state of the charging circuit. A good battery will read 13 to 13.5 volts at rest, which should rise to 14 to 14.5 once the engine is running. Test again under load, with the headlights, indicators, heater fan, etc., on. The revs may need lifting slightly off idle with an alternator under load, and even more when a dynamo is fitted.

Engine/front subframe/gearbox mounts

The engine has a mount at the bellhousing and another just visible under the radiator. Look for splits or other signs of deterioration particularly if oil soaked. Underneath there may be one or two tie bars

Tie bar rubbers split and, in some cases, the bar can pull clean off the head.

depending on age, and the same faults may be found. The last brace is mounted between the head and the body and again suffers from splitting rubber bushes, or the mounting bolt can snap clean off the head. The front subframe has a pair of teardrop-shaped mounts which bolt to the front panel, and a pair at the back which attach to car floor; the same checks will again show up any defects.

Carburettor   4️⃣   3️⃣   2️⃣   1️⃣

There will either be a single or a pair of SU units fitted, with a remote float chamber on the early cars, or an integral one thereafter. All variants are reliable and fairly long-lived, and require little maintenance other than keeping the dashpot topped up and a squirt of oil on linkages and pivot points. After a considerable mileage the piston can score which leads to flat spots as you accelerate, and the spindles wear with the subsequent air leak leading to an irregular idle. With the engine turned off, try lifting the spindle in relation to the body and check for movement. Re-bushing is possible but replacement is easier.

Check that there are no leaks from the carb.

On earlier cars the carb body is connected to the remote float by a small pipe, make sure that it's not leaking as fuel can drop straight down onto the exhaust. Later cars have single-point fuel injection, then right at the end of production multi-point. These systems are pretty reliable but any misfires or running problems will take more time to locate and rectify than with a carb-equipped car. Minor irregularity of idle may just indicate a dirty throttle body requiring a clean out, but could also be a distortion in the body, faulty senders (in particular, the temperature one), or wear in the flap pivots, so diagnosis is not going to be immediate.

Exhaust   4 3 2 1

This is the lowest point on an already ground-hugging car, so it's susceptible to knocks. It can fracture at the downpipe if the engine mounts and head steady are worn out or if it's not correctly attached to the gearbox. Listen for the telltale burbling from gases leaking from the inaccessible and hard to seal joint at the manifold. Cars fitted with catalytic converters may have an irritating buzzing rattle from the unit when revved, which may be a sign of the internal core breaking up. This can happen while the 'cat' is still fully functional, but it's hard to live with and replacement is the only answer. Check the end of the tailpipe on all cars, as it can give an indication of the state of tune and the amount of engine wear. Any deposits should be light grey in colour. Darker ones which can be wiped easily onto the finger but are relatively dry indicate a rich mixture; dark, wet and sticky ones which smear and adhere to your fingers probably means that the car is burning oil, which is bad news on all versions; plus it may have damaged the 'cat' on late cars as well.

Shock absorbers   4 3 2 1

Standard hydraulic shocks can be tested by bouncing the car, they should only allow one and a half oscillations before it's at rest again. The only other test is a visual one for corroded sleeves, split bushes, and signs of oil leakage. Hydrolastic cars rely on fluid to provide the spring, and many people say it provides a better ride. Check for leaks at each displacer unit mounted in approximately the same place as the cones on dry cars, and lift the rubber boot to check for leaks. The system can be pumped back up assuming there are no problems, but the number of facilities offering this once common service is dropping. Make sure to check all the pipework on hydrolastic Minis for rust, damage or fluid leaks.

Test drive

This should last at least 15 minutes and include as many different road types as possible. Make sure you're happy with the seat position, mirror adjustment, and the layout of all the controls before you set off, as your thoughts must be concentrated on how the car performs, not in fumbling around trying to find a particular button.

Braking check   4 3 2 1

Before driving off it's worth checking the state of the brake pedal, which should be firm under foot. Apply a gentle pressure and try to push it down very slowly, if it sinks under this soft but constant load, then the seals in the master cylinder are shot. This can be double-checked by taking your foot off and quickly reapplying it, which will immediately give a firm pedal again. If the car has a servo fitted, pump the pedal and hold the pressure on then start the engine, the pedal should drop half an inch or so instantly if the servo is working correctly.

Starting/warning lights [4] [3] [2] [1]

Turn the key and make sure that the oil (amber colour) and ignition light (red) go on. If cold the choke will have to be pulled out, it then twists to lock. Hot or cold, the A-series engine should willingly burst into life. Make sure that the starter is not noisy in operation; a clanging noise as it meets the flywheel may mean ring gear wear requiring an engine strip. If a separate oil pressure gauge is fitted this should immediately rise to $70lb/in^2$ or so, dropping to 50 to 60lb once the engine is warmed and running normally. At idle and hot it should not drop below 15lb. Low oil pressure or a flickering warning light probably means wear in the bottom end. Once on the move make sure that the speedo works, as the cable is extremely awkward to change on a Mini.

Clutch [4] [3] [2] [1]

The pedal should feel firm and bite halfway up its travel. Too high and the clutch is worn, too low and it needs adjustment or there's a problem with the hydraulic circuit, or the crank has lots of end float. Mini clutches can be rather sharp if you're not used to it, but it should be free from judder which would indicate oil contamination.

Gearbox [4] [3] [2] [1]

The Mini gearbox is pretty robust, but sharing its oil with the engine was never going to do it any favours if servicing was neglected. Gear selection should be easy, if a little notchy, especially into first. Make sure that the car doesn't pop out of gear under a sudden load, which should be checked by deliberately accelerating and decelerating sharply in each gear. Ensure that the synchromesh system (not fitted to first on early cars) is working, particularly coming down the box; weak or damaged rings will cause screaming and crunching as you try to go into a lower gear with the engine spinning quickly, particularly the drop from third to second. There will always be a slight whine from the box which will be worse in first gear, but it should never be strident at any time or accompanied by a feeling of roughness. Take extra time if you're unsure about any noise emanating from the box, as repair is awkward and expensive.

Auto box [4] [3] [2] [1]

This will be less refined than those found in more modern cars, although Minis post-1979 are better than the early ones. A screech whilst pulling away is bad news, as is a reluctance to take up drive promptly after each change. The change point should be reasonably smooth, any heavy clonking spells trouble. Try the kick-down mechanism; the drop to a lower gear should be quick and provide an immediate increase in speed, although these autos are lethargic compared to a manual. Be critical of defects with an auto, as a reconditioned box is about three times the price of a stick shift one, and most suppliers will insist on a torque converter change at the same time to comply with the warranty.

Steering on the move [4] [3] [2] [1]

The steering on a Mini should be light and precise. Any vibration coming back up through the wheel could be from out-of-balance tyres, worn suspension, track rod ends, or the rack itself. Your static check should have picked up on any problems with the last three before the test drive. If it happens only under braking, then the likely candidate is a warped front disc.

Brakes on the road   [4] [3] [2] [1]

On the move, the brakes should pull up in a straight line. If they have a bias to one side the caliper may be sticking or, if it's a drum-braked car, one of the wheel cylinders may be leaking. Having said that, front drums can be a pain to set up to pull straight, particularly if cheap cylinders and shoes have been fitted. The next time you stop, apply the handbrake and try to drive off. You will probably find that the handbrake is useless, which is fairly common, or that the back end drops on one side as the other isn't working, thanks to a seized quadrant or cable. This exercise may also make a worn clutch slip if the handbrake is working to any extent.

Noises and smells   [4] [3] [2] [1]

A Mini is a noisy beast compared to more modern cars, but certain specific noises may stand out and indicate problems. A clicking or knocking with the steering on full lock will almost certainly be worn-out CV joints. A knock which only occurs once under sudden acceleration or deceleration will probably be the engine mounts or the engine steady bar (there may be two on some models). A squeaking noise from the front end over bumps is probably worn cups in the upper suspension arms that the trumpets sit in.

Crabbing   [4] [3] [2] [1]

The last check is to see if the car runs straight and true, and this may involve following it down a straight road and ensuring that the bodyshell sits squarely to the direction of travel and the wheels. Poor repairs, accident damage, or even structural weakness can leave the car with the subframes twisted in relation to the shell, so check that you cannot see one side of the car more clearly when travelling directly behind it. This defect is pretty obvious, and will take a lot of money, time and skill to rectify, so if it's apparent it's best to move on and find another Mini.

Evaluation procedure

Add up the total points. Score: 172 = excellent; 129 = good; 86 = average; 43 = poor.

Cars scoring over 120 will be completely useable and will require only maintenance and care to keep in condition. Cars scoring between 43 and 87 will require serious restoration (at much the same cost regardless of score). Cars scoring between 88 and 119 will require very careful assessment of necessary repair/restoration costs in order to reach a realistic value.

10 Auctions
– sold! Another way to buy your dream

Although mainstream Minis are not yet a regular sight at classic car auctions, unlike early Coopers, their burgeoning appeal and rising values will undoubtedly see that situation change over time, so it's worth a moment to consider another route to your dream purchase.

Auction pros and cons
Pros: Prices tend to be lower than those asked by either dealers or private sellers, so it could be your chance to pick up a bargain. The auctioneers have usually checked out the legal status of the car, and relevant paperwork can often be viewed before the sale.

Cons: There's often little opportunity to inspect the cars fully, and they cannot be driven. Many cars end up in auctions as they require some work, the trick is to spot exactly what that may be and factor it in to your bids. It's also very easy to get caught in an upward spiral of bidding and spend too much. There may also be a buyer's premium to add to the hammer price.

Which auction?
Classic car magazines have listings of forthcoming auctions, and most auctioneers have a website detailing the vehicles, usually accompanied by a photograph. There may be details of previous sales and the amounts reached by each lot, which will give you an idea of the state of the market.

Catalogue, entry fee and payment details
Entry to the sale and any viewing days is often included in the purchase price of the catalogue. This document will also list each lot with a brief description of the car, any paperwork, such as service history, MoT, etc., and mileage. It may also include a guide price which the auctioneers expect it to make, and any premiums due if sold. Once the hammer has fallen, payment of a deposit is usually expected immediately, with any outstanding balance paid within 24 hours. Read the catalogue carefully about payment methods as auction houses vary in what they will accept, and they may charge extra for the use of your flexible friend. Whatever payment method you choose, the car will not be released until cleared payment has been made, and if you delay in sorting it all out, a storage charge may be added.

Buyer's premium
A buyer's premium will almost certainly be added to the final hammer price; remember to factor it into your bidding. There may also be a state or other local tax.

Viewing
It's likely that there will be a set viewing time either immediately before the sale or, preferably, a couple of days in advance. Ask for the bonnet and boot to be opened and the engine started, plus check out all available paperwork for the car. It may be possible to have the car jacked up to check suspension, steering, etc., so take advantage of any opportunity to examine the vehicle as closely as possible.

Bidding

Auctions are exciting, especially when several people are after the same car, and it's all too easy to get swept along in the euphoria of it all. So, before you start down this potentially expensive road, decide on the maximum amount you're willing to pay and stick to it. If you're unfamiliar with auction procedure get there early, register to bid, then settle back and watch how other people do it. When your car arrives, bid early so the auctioneer knows where you are, he/she will keep coming back to see your reaction to other bids. If it's time to duck out make it very clear, a vigorous shake of the head should be enough. If you win, your card number will be taken and you will have to go and pay your deposit. If the car you want fails to sell because it hasn't reached its reserve, it may still be worth going to the office and registering your interest, as the auctioneers may contact the owner with your offer to see if they wish to sell.

Successful bid

With the car secured and hopefully paid for the next issue is getting it home. If you cannot drive the vehicle (no insurance or MoT, for example), either hire a trailer or arrange for one of the many transport firms to shift it for you; the auction office should have a list of suitable companies for you to contact. Some sales also offer immediate short term insurance cover but this is rarely the most cost-effective way of dealing with the problem; a phone call to your usual broker will almost certainly sort out something cheaper.

Internet auctions

There are undoubtedly bargains to be had via internet auction sites, but the overriding rule is never to buy anything unless you've seen it in the metal or it's so cheap that any spares gleaned from the car would be worth more than you paid. As usual, distance comes into play here, so try to limit your search to an area close to home. Once again, it's possible to get carried away bidding, so set a limit and don't be tempted beyond it in the last few minutes of the auction when things hot up. It's very hard to get your money back if you're misled and, unfortunately, there are also cases of outright fraud, so be careful.

Auctioneers

Barrett-Jackson www.barrett-jackson.com
Bonhams www.bonhams.com
British Car Auctions www.british-car-auctions.co.uk
Cheffins www.cheffins.co.uk
Christies www.christies.com
Coys www.coys.co.uk
H&H www.classic-auctions.co.uk
RM www.rmauctions.com
Shannons www.shannons.com.au
Silver www.silverauctions.com
eBay www.ebay.com/www.ebay.co.uk

11 Paperwork
– correct documentation is essential!

The paper trail
With the Mini now firmly in the classic and collector sector, the amount of paperwork available to document the history of any prospective purchase is very important. Old receipts for work done, particularly from known specialists, will make the vehicle more attractive to future buyers, so never throw anything away.

Registration documents
Virtually every country has a system or recording vehicle and owner details on a single form, the log book or V5C in the UK, Pink Slip in the USA, for example. Check that all the information on the form is correct and that it relates to the person selling the car and the car you're actually looking at. If the vehicle is registered overseas complications may arise, but within the EEC, things are a lot easier than they used to be. Check with your relevant licensing authority beforehand, though, as registration can be a long-winded and potentially expensive process in some countries.

Roadworthiness certificate
Wherever you live there's likely to be a regular test to check the roadworthiness of your car and the amount of pollution it's creating. In the UK a certificate is issued when the vehicle passes the annual test, permitting the car's use for 12 months. A valid certificate is essential with your purchase unless you're specifically buying a restoration project. Old certificates are often kept by owners, and this helps show accumulated mileage and adds to the general history of the car.

Service records and old MoT certificates can verify mileage and should be kept safe.

Road fund licence
Virtually every country has a form of tax that must be paid in order to use your vehicle on the road. There's often a sticker or disc that must be displayed in the windscreen to prove compliance and the dates of validity. If the proposed purchase isn't taxed make sure that any other relevant laws have been adhered to. For example, in the UK a SORN declaration (Statutory Off Road Notification) must be made or the owner is fined. If the car has been laid up for a very long time, it may not have the latest registration document and so avoided this paperwork, but as the new owner you will have to sort it out.

Certificates of authenticity

Minis built after 1969 cannot be supplied with a Heritage Certificate like many other British classics, however a letter confirming the build date can be obtained.

Valuation certificate

If the car in question is insured under a classic car policy, the owner may have had to arrange an independent inspection and valuation to satisfy the insurers. Ask to see it, and for a copy if you buy the car. Do not take the opinions expressed in the document as fact, as some specialists can be lenient in appraisals for insurance purposes, but it should help to confirm some of the points that you've spotted whilst working your way through the inspection laid out in this book. If there's no certificate and you need one, then the first port of call is the owner's club which should have an officer capable of providing the relevant information and putting you in touch with someone able to inspect the car and issue a certificate.

Service history

It is unlikely that you'll find a Mini with a full dealer service history unless it's a very late model, but records of regular care from a specialist are just as valuable, and even those from a local garage are better than nothing. Many cars are looked after by their owners, so ask how often the oil was changed, for example (and every 3000 miles is what you want to hear), and the quality and specification of the lubricant used. Even the brand of oil filter chosen can give an indication of the amount of care taken during servicing. A knowledgeable seller should be able to answer servicing questions promptly and in some detail. Any receipts for parts or work are useful and should be retained.

Original handbooks and other period paperwork are interesting historically, and become more sought-after once a car is recognised as a classic.

Restoration photographs

Most people take photos during a restoration for their own pleasure, but they also know it will ultimately enhance the value of the car when it's time to sell. Make sure the car in the shots is actually the one you're looking at, compare backgrounds if it's a home restoration, or look for areas where fresh work can be readily verified. Make sure that the seller will hand over the photos, or a least copies or scans if you buy the car; they'll be just as valuable to you in the future.

12 What's it worth to you?
– let your head rule your heart!

Having worked your way through the inspection chapters you should have a good idea of your proposed car's condition, whether a total basket case but suitable for restoration, or a clean useable car ready to drive away. If you've done your homework and checked the price guides in classic car and Mini-specific magazines, and gone to a few shows or kept an eye on the internet ads for a time, you should be able to decide if that condition merits the price being asked.

The structure or mechanical solidity of the vehicle may not be the only factor to take into account, though, as other issues like rarity also have a bearing. The time, effort and money needed to resurrect a 1980s Mini may not be reflected in its final value, but the same amount lavished on an early Cooper or a Mk 1 Saloon might be money very well spent. As a general rule, the newer the car the higher score it needs to have accumulated using the *Essential Buyer's Guide* points system to make it worth its money.

The Mini was an austere machine throughout most of its life, and the factory fitted few luxuries. A multitude of aftermarket suppliers sprang up to offer a bewildering range of accessories, particularly during the 1960s. Some of these extras now command a hefty premium as they're sought after to add the finishing touches to a perfect period restoration.

Less universally admired is customising, and buying a heavily-modified car is a risky option as opinions can be divided on the success of some alterations. Unleaded heads, mild tuning, or a set of alloy wheels may be a good selling point as they would probably have little impact on insurance rates, but other modifications like race cams or extreme cubic capacities may turn the car into a sales liability. This is particularly true in the case of older Minis that have been rebuilt to modern specifications, work that may not raise an eyebrow when done to an '80s Saloon may

Bolt-on goodies like this fibreglass flip front may be desirable to some, but could put off twice as many.

not elicit the same reaction if carried out on a Mk 1, where the main appeal for most people may well be originality.

Finally, once you've decided how much the car is worth to you, never be afraid of haggling, list some of the defects that you will undoubtedly have found as justification for a price reduction, it may not work, but the worst that can happen is that you'll end up paying the full asking price. Dealers, in particular, are more flexible, as they'll have built in a fair margin to begin with to cover warranty work or rectification of minor problems pre-sale.

13 Do you really want to restore?
– it'll take longer and cost more than you think

The idea of restoring a car is very tempting on many levels, especially if you do it yourself, and little can match the sense of pride in seeing a wreck returned to the road through your own endeavours. The other alternative is to choose a professional to do the work for you, which is less fun and a lot more expensive. Either route will throw up some serious issues that need careful consideration before making your final decision.

If you opt for doing it yourself, be ruthless in assessing your real abilities, can you successfully chop out rot and replace it all with new steel without distorting some vital section? Will your paintwork come up to scratch? How many engines have you successfully rebuilt? The skills needed to sort out these problems can be gained by most people, but have you enough spare time to acquire them? Have you got the space, the tools, or enough obliging friends who will lend them to you? Finally, it's very easy to underestimate just how long is needed to restore a car properly, so have a chat with someone who has done a Mini already. If they're honest they're likely to tell you that it's best to double the amount of time and money you think it will all take to see the car completed. This list of potential troubles is not an attempt to put you off, but the small ads in Mini magazines are usually well padded with 'unfinished projects', and you don't want your dream to end up that way, particularly as it usually entails a financial loss to boot.

On the bodywork side there's an alternative to long hours with the welder, and that is to buy a newly-made British Heritage shell, which can even be supplied ready painted leaving just the mechanical and trim bits to bolt on. The time factor associated with a DIY restoration can also be cut down by doing a rolling restoration, but this has its own inherent problems as jobs do not always conveniently fit into the slots you've allocated for them, and part restored cars that look a mess tend to attract unwanted attention on today's roads. Paintwork doesn't fit this scenario very well either, so that at least would really have to be done in one go, unless you want to deal with soggy filler, peeling primer and ingrained dirt on every panel.

If you decide to have a professional do the work, make your exact requirements crystal clear and commit them to paper; there's always the chance of disappointment. One area where you definitely don't want any surprises is the amount it's all going to cost, so always get a written quote stating precisely what will be done, for how much, and by which date. Try and get something included to the effect that the final amount will not exceed the quotation by more than 10 per cent. Before entering an agreement, check out the firm's reputation, and look at some of its previous work, especially the most recent. Speak to other people who have used the company about their experiences; both good and bad. Most established Mini specialists will have a waiting list so it could be some time before your car reaches the head of the queue.

Last, but certainly not least, compare the price of cars that are already restored against the likely amount you'll have to stump up to get yours done, there may be a financial advantage in simply buying one 'off the shelf,' with the added bonus that you can enjoy the Mini experience straightaway.

There's no need to worry about the availability of replacement panels for a Mini.

You'll have to lay out a significant amount of money on tools and equipment if you want to restore.

Fading

This afflicts red paint hues more frequently than other shades, but a lack of paint care can see it affect all shades in the end. Either way, the situation may be rescued by T-Cut or a similar compound, but if that fails to restore the shine a repaint is in order.

Bubbling

This is a result of rust forming under the paint layer (or filler) and swelling up. The extent of the corrosion is always greater than the visible area, and when the old paint is removed thin threads of rust will be found creeping out from the centre of the problem. Removal of all the old paint from around the affected area and rectification of the rust problem is the only answer.

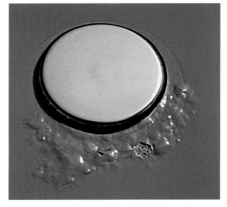

Paint tends to blister as rust creeps underneath, usually starting where there are holes in the panel.

Crazing/cracking

These two problems share similar roots: inadequate paint preparation, a reaction to old material left on the metal, contamination of the primer, or the paint was applied over filler which hadn't cured properly. To make sure that the problem doesn't return, take the surface back down to bare metal before filling and repainting.

Orange peel

This is a result of too much paint being applied, and the surface really does resemble orange peel. This can usually be rectified by flatting off with fine wet and dry paper to

Crazing is unsightly and impossible to sort out without going back to bare metal.

level the surface, followed by buffing. This is labour-intensive, however, so will be expensive if you're paying someone else to do it.

Micro blistering

These are tiny blisters of solvent or water trapped under the new paint, and as such are not easily treated without stripping it all off and starting again.

Silicone dimples

If the car has had a quick respray or other paintwork, then silicone

Micro blistering is time-consuming and expensive to rectify.

residues from the workplace can be left under the new paint, which then looks like little puddles in the surface. These can only be rectified by repainting.

Peeling paint/lacquer

If the primer has been inadequately flatted or has a contaminant on the surface the top coat will not adhere properly and can flake off. If this happens to a clear over base finish then the whole lot will have to be taken back down and redone. Solid coats may respond to a localised repair.

Flaking paint is unsightly, but at least there's the possibility of flatting back to sound paint and blowing in.

Dents

The panel work on a Mini is very thin and dents easily; it's also very hard to fill properly to disguise them. If the damage is shallow and the paint unbroken then one of the specialist dent removal firms may be able to help.

15 Problems due to lack of use

– just like their owners, Minis need exercise!

Hydraulic problems

Brake fluid is hydroscopic and attracts water which promotes internal rusting of metal components. Expect seized wheel cylinders and caliper pistons if the car hasn't been moved for a long period, and even a short period could produce enough contamination to give a spongy pedal.

Coolant problems

The cast iron block will rust internally if there's a low concentration of anti-freeze, as it also contains corrosion inhibitors. Flushing will remove light silting; shifting heavier deposits will require chemical treatment.

Brake components don't like inactivity; they corrode internally and seize.

Electrical problems

Alternators, dynamos, starters, electric fuel pumps and mechanical voltage regulators do not like standing. Corrosion builds up on exposed brushes and their tracks, and the points in pumps and regulators fur up. No battery will stand long-term inactivity well, and recharging will fail to revive them if the debris usually held in suspension in the electrolyte has settled and shorted out the plates. Wiring connections oxidise and frequently require separating and cleaning, as do bulb holders.

Electrical components often fail quickly once back in use.

Oil contamination

Engine oil picks up several nasty contaminants when in use, including acids, and if the car has been used regularly for short trips, water from condensation can be a problem. When the vehicle is then left unused, these promote rusting and deterioration on bearing surfaces and on cylinder walls. Change the oil as soon as the car can be run and once again a short time after the vehicle has been put back on the road. This is particularly important with a Mini as the gearbox will not tolerate poor quality oil.

Tyres

Tyres have a finite life of around five years, by which time they'll have started to harden and deteriorate. If left sitting unused, and particularly if under-inflated, there's a real chance that they'll go out of shape and retain that deformity for good. Check the sidewalls carefully for cracking.

Exhaust

All petrol cars produce condensation until they have reached operating temperature, which then collects in the exhaust and rots it from the inside out. Cars left to stand usually gain more from the atmosphere, so expect anything that has been sitting for any length of time to have a well corroded exhaust

Tyres last for just 5 years or so; less if they've been left under-inflated.

regardless of how good it may look from the outside.

Greasing points

Radius arms and front suspension top arms require regular doses of clean grease to keep them in good order. All grease hardens when left and loses its ability to lubricate properly. Pump fresh stuff in as soon as possible, ensuring all the old crusty gunge has been fully expelled. Remove the CV joint boots and clean and re-pack those as well.

Stale fuel/pump problems

Modern unleaded fuel goes stale more

Exhausts suffer from internal corrosion, and, although they may look fine externally, are often wafer thin.

readily than the old leaded variety, leaving a sticky deposit when it evaporates. This clogs jets and clings to the float bowl where it becomes a hard, semi-fossilised

coating if left too long. Any car that has been unused for more than 12 months would probably benefit from a carburettor strip and clean. No fuel pump likes standing for extended periods either, and sometimes they need back filling to prime them before they function properly again, although the diaphragm (mechanical type) may be beyond saving if it has been allowed to dry out completely and then left.

Petrol pumps don't like extended periods of idleness, so be prepared to replace them on restoration projects.

16 The Community
– key people, organisations and companies in the Mini world

UK clubs
British Mini Club
www.britishminiclub.co.uk
Tel 01384 897779
Email info@britishminiclub.co.uk

Mini Cooper Club
www.minicooperclub.com
Email postmaster@minicooperclub.com

Mini Cooper Register
www.minicooper.org
Email membership@minicooper.org

Mini Special Register
www.brmmbrmm.com/
minispecialregister
Tel 07966 0142944
Email minispecial@bushinternet.com

National Mini Owners Club
www.miniownersclub.co.uk
Tel 01543 257956
Email mini@club.freeserve.co.uk

Continental clubs
B Mini Club of Belgium
www.miniclubofbelgium.be

CH Berne Mini Club
www.mini.org/bmc

DK Mini Club Denmark
www.mini-club-denmark.dk

F Esprit Mini Team
www.esprit-mini.net

D Mini Register Germany
www.miniregister.org

I Mini Club Italy
www.miniclassic.it

YU Minimanija Serbia
www.minimanija.co.yu

S Mini Club Sweden
www.miniclubsweden.com

USA
Mini Car Club of America
www.minicca.org

Mini Owners of America LA
www.moala.org

Mini Owners San Francisco
www.moasf.com

Canada
Toronto Mini Club
www.torontominiclub.com

Vancouver Mini Club
www.vancouverminiclub.ca

Australia
Mini Car Club NSW
www.miniclub.com.au

Mini Club South Aus
www.miniclubsa.asa.au/

Mini Car Club Tasmania
www.minitas.org.au

New Zealand
Mini Car Club Auckland
www.minis-auckland.org.nz

Mini Cooper Club NZ
www.minicooper.org.nz

Suppliers are listed in alphabetical order. Inclusion is not a recommendation; please treat any omissions as accidental. Speak to owners in your area for up-to-date information on the best business to meet your requirements.

Parts suppliers: European

Anglo Parts Belgium
www.angloparts.com
Tel 0032 15 42 37 83
Email sales.belgium@angloparts.com

BL Empire (B)
www.blempire.com
Tel 0032 89 723 397

British Motor Heritage (UK)
www.bmh-ltd.com
Tel 0044 (0) 1993 707200
Email info@bmh-ltd.com

DSN Classics (UK)
www.dsnclassics.co.uk
Tel 0044 (0) 1953 455551
Email sales@dsnclassics.co.uk

Hadrian Panels (UK)
www.carpanels.co.uk
Tel/Email see website for regional contacts

Huddersfield Spares (UK)
www.minispares-online.co.uk
Tel 0044 (0) 148465 8524
Email sales@minispares-online.co.uk

Jon Speed Racing (UK)
www.jonspeed4minis.co.uk
Tel 0044 (0) 2476 351495
Email info@jonspeedracing.co.uk

Just Minis (UK)
www.justminis.net
Tel 0044 (0) 1268 799963
Email justminis@btinternet.com

Loco Classic Parts (NL)
www.lococlassiccarparts.nl
Tel 0031 (0) 499 377 501
Email info@lococlassiccarparts.nl

M – Machine (UK)
www.m-machine.co.uk
Tel 0044 (0) 1325 381300
Email sales@m-machine.co.uk

Mini Mail (UK)
www.minimail.co.uk
Tel 0044 (0) 1989 720 111
Email spares@minimail.co.uk

Mini Mania (D)
www.mini-mania.tv
Tel 0049 (0) 4402 82044
Email info@mini-mania.tv

Mini Spares (UK)
www.minispares.com
Tel 0044 (0) 1707 607700
Email sales@minispares.com

Mini Speed (UK)
www.minispeed.co.uk
Tel 0044 (0) 1932 400 567
Email sales@minispeed.co.uk

Mini Sport (UK)
www.minisport.com
Tel 0044 (0) 1282 778731
Email sales@minisport.com

US parts suppliers

Mini City
www.minicityltd.com
Tel 585-872-6560
Email MiniCityUS@aol.com

Mini Mania
www.minimania.com
Tel 530-470-8300

Mini Motors
www.minimotors.com

Australian suppliers

Mini Sport
www.minisport.com.au

Tel 08-8177-1275
Email sales@minisport.com.au

Canadian suppliers
A Grade
www.agradepanels.com.au
Tel (03) 5780 1300
agradepanels@iprimus.com.au

Mr. Mini
www.mrmini.com
Tel 1-866-628-6464

Books
Mini 50 years
Rob Golding
ISBN 978-0760326275 (Motorbooks)

Complete Classic Mini
Chris Rees
ISBN 978-1899870608 (Motor Racing
Publications)

*Mini – A celebration of Britain's best
loved small car*
Graham Robson
ISBN 978-1844253265 (J H Haynes)

Anatomy of the Works Minis
Brian Moylan
ISBN 978-1903706039 (Veloce)

Mini Cooper/Mini Cooper S
Graham Robson
ISBN 978-1845841836 (Veloce)

*Maximum Mini – The essential book of
cars based on the original Mini*
Jeroen Booij
ISBN 978-1845841546 (Veloce)

Original Mini Cooper
John Parnell
ISBN 978-0760312285 (Motorbooks
International)

Mini Cooper: The Real Thing
ISBN 1874105227 (Veloce Publishing)

Magazines
Mini World
www.miniworld.co.uk

Mini Magazine
www.minimag.co.uk

17 Vital statistics
– essential data at your fingertips

Technical specifications of selected cars from each decade
The '60s 848cc Saloon, 34bhp@5500rpm, weight 1380lb, top speed 72mph
The '70s 998cc Saloon, 39bhp@5250rpm, weight 1400lb, top speed 75mph
1275 Clubman GT, 59bhp@5300rpm, weight 1555lb, top speed 90mph
The '90s 1275 multi-point injection, 63bhp@5500rpm, weight 1610lb, top
speed 88mph

Timeline – the major events in the Mini's development
1959 The Mini is launched under the names Austin Mini 7 and the Morris Mini Minor, both 848cc.
1960 Van and Estate versions are launched.
1961 A Pick-up joins the list of available variants, along with the sporty Cooper.
1962 Austin 7 version renamed Austin Mini and the fake wood of the first estates disappears leaving the body all metal.
1963 The Cooper S arrives making the Mini a genuine 100mph car.
1964 Hydrolastic suspension fitted.
1965 An automatic option is made available.
1967 Various changes herald the arrival of the Mk 2 version of the Mini.
1968 Hydrolastic suspension dropped.
1969 Mk 3 body shell arrives with internal hinges, along with a longer nosed version, the Clubman in both Saloon and Estate versions. Austin and Morris badges dropped in favour of simply Mini.
1971 Link-up with Cooper came to an end.
1976 The Mini Limited Edition is launched, the first of many. The body is now the Mk 4 incarnation with changes to the front subframe mounts.
1979 The Mini 1100 special arrives with the 1098cc Clubman engine and 10in alloy wheels.
1980 The Clubman is axed from the range and the Mini City is launched.
1982 The Mini Mayfair is added as a more luxurious option to the City, it has headrests and a radio. The Van and Pick-ups reach the end of the road.
1984 12in wheels and disc brakes are fitted across the range which turns the Mini into the Mk 5 version. A silver Mayfair is produced to celebrate 25 years of production.
1985-89 This period was a seemingly endless parade of 'Special Editions', in launch order they were: The Mini Ritz, Chelsea, Piccadilly, Park Lane, Advantage, Red Hot, Jet Black, Designer, Racing, Flame, Rose, Sky, and then finally in 1989, the Mini 30 to celebrate another production milestone.
1990 The 30 and the MG Metro were combined to make the Rover Mini Cooper. The special editions continued to be churned out with the Racing Green, Flame Red, Check Mate and Studio 2.
1991 Single-point injection arrived as did 13in wheels, plus a Cabriolet version which was originally only going to be another special edition but continued as a mainstream Rover product until 1996.
1992 The Mini British Open Classic and the *Italian Job* special editions entered the showrooms. The Mayfair gets the 1275cc engine.

1994   The milestone of 35 years production was celebrated with the Mini 35, plus two different version of the Mini Cooper Monte Carlo in January and July which had spotlights to go with the usual cosmetic changes.

1996   Multi-point injection and a change of position for the radiator make these Minis the Mk 7.

1998-99 The specials kept being churned out, this batch being the Rover Mini Paul Smith, the Mini Cooper Sports, the Cooper S Touring, the Mini Cooper Sport 5, the Mini Cooper S Works, the John Cooper LE, the Cooper Sport 500 LE and last, but not least, the Rover Mini 40.

2000   The last Mini rolled off the Longbridge production line.

The Essential Buyer's Guide™

The Essential Buyer's Guide
ALFA ROMEO GIULIA
GT COUPE
978-1-904788-69-0

The Essential Buyer's Guide
ALFA ROMEO GIULIA
SPIDER
978-1-904788-98-0

The Essential Buyer's Guide
BMW
GS
978-1-84584-135-5

The Essential Buyer's Guide
BSA
Bantam
All models 1948 to 1971
978-1-84584-165-2

The Essential Buyer's Guide
BSA
500&650 Twins
A7, A10, A50 & A65, 1946 to 1973
978-1-84584-136-2

The Essential Buyer's Guide
CITROËN
2CV
978-1-845840-99-0

The Essential Buyer's Guide
CITROËN
DS & ID
All models 1966 to 1975
978-1-84584-138-6

The Essential Buyer's Guide
FIAT
500 & 600 1955 to 1982
Saloons/Sedans, Multipla, Giardiniera & 126
978-1-84584-147-8

The Essential Buyer's Guide
JAGUAR
E-type
3.8 & 4.2 litre
978-1-904788-85-0

The Essential Buyer's Guide
JAGUAR
E-type
V12 5.3 litre
978-1845840-77-8

The Essential Buyer's Guide
Jaguar/Daimler
XJ
978-1-84584-200-0

The Essential Buyer's Guide
JAGUAR
XJ-S
All 6- and 12-cylinder models 1975 to 1996
978-1-84584-161-4

The Essential Buyer's Guide
JAGUAR/DAIMLER
XJ6, XJ12 & Sovereign
All Jaguar/Daimler/VDP models 1986 to 1992
978-1-845841-19-5

The Essential Buyer's Guide
Triumph
TR6
978-1-845840-26-6

The Essential Buyer's Guide
MERCEDES-BENZ PAGODA
230, 250 & 280SL
W113 series Roadsters & Coupés 1963 to 1971
978-1-845841-13-3

The Essential Buyer's Guide
MERCEDES-BENZ
280-560SL & SLC
W107 series Roadsters & Coupés 1971 to 1989
978-1-845841-07-2

The Essential Buyer's Guide
MG
MGB MGB GT
978-1-845840-29-7

The Essential Buyer's Guide
MORRIS
MINOR & 1000
Saloons, Travellers & Convertibles 1952 to 1971
978-1-845841-01-0

The Essential Buyer's Guide
PORSCHE
928
All models
978-1-904788-70-6

The Essential Buyer's Guide
ROLLS-ROYCE
SILVER SHADOW
BENTLEY
T-SERIES
including Corniche, Camargue, Silver Shadow II & Bentley T 2, 1965 to 1996
978-1-84584-146-1

The Essential Buyer's Guide
SUBARU
Impreza
All turbo models 1994 to 2007
978-1-84584-163-8

The Essential Buyer's Guide
TRIUMPH
BONNEVILLE
978-1-84584-134-8

The Essential Buyer's Guide
MINI
978-1-84584-204-8

The Essential Buyer's Guide
VOLKSWAGEN
BEETLE
978-1-904788-72-0

The Essential Buyer's Guide
VOLKSWAGEN
BUS
978-1-845840-22-8

The Essential Buyer's Guide
Volkswagen
GOLF GTI
Mk1 and Mk2 models including Cabriolet, Mk1s & Mk2s
978-1-84584-188-1

The Essential Buyer's Guide
Jaguar/Daimler
XJ40
978-1-84584-192-8

The Essential Buyer's Guide
Triumph
STAG
978-1-845842-70-3

£9.99*/ $19.95*

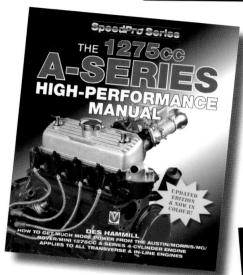
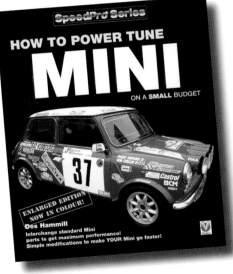

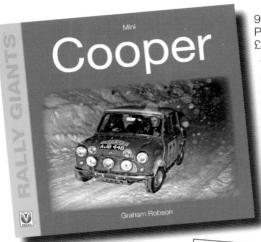

978-1-84584-183-6
Paperback + flaps • 128 pages •
£14.99 • 100 pictures

This book describes the birth,
development, and rallying career
of the BMC Mini-Cooper/Mini-
Cooper in the 1960s, providing a
compact and authoritative history of
where, when and how it became so
important to the sport.

978-1-84584-154-6
Hardback • £24.95 • 128 pages

Mini derivatives changed the
specialist motoring market
completely in the early sixties,
and new designs kept it busy
for nearly four decades. From
the well-known Mini Marcos
to the very obscure Coldwell
GT, almost 60 cars are
researched, described and
photographed in this book.

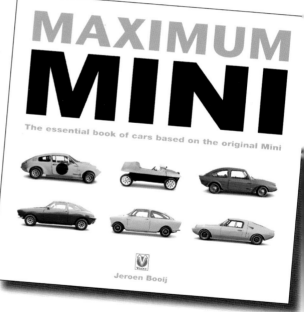

**All prices subject to change • P&P extra • email info@veloce.co.uk
or call +44 (0)1305 260068 for more information**

978-1-904788-68-3
Hardback • £24.99 •
192 pages

Three Competitions
Department Managers
reveal the inner workings
& long-held secrets of one
of the most prominent
motorsport teams
Britain has ever seen.
Internal memos, highs
& lows, and politics. Be
prepared, much of this is
sensational!

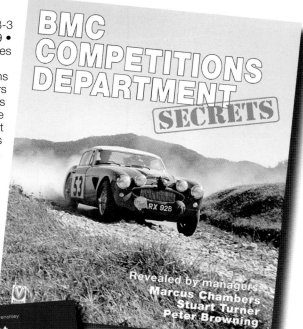

978-1-845840-87-7
Hardback • £29.99 • 192 pages

The story of the Works Mini's
'second coming' to compete
in modern rallying and racing.
Includes previously unpublished
photos of the car's development,
copies of Rover's internal
documents, and pages from the
road books of top rallies.

Index